DYI
C000152530

By the same author
Turning the Tide with Alan Wilkinson (1980)
Pastors under Pressure (1989)

Dynamic Leadership

Making It Work for You and Your Church

PAUL BEASLEY-MURRAY

MARC
Eastbourne

Biblical quotations are from the New International Version,
copyright © International Bible Society 1973, 1978, 1984.
RSV = Revised Standard Version
Copyrighted 1946, 1952, © 1971, 1973 by the Division of
Education and Ministry of the National Council of the
Churches of Christ in the USA

Cover design by W. James Hammond
Front cover photo: Zefa Picture Library

British Library Cataloguing in Publication Data

Beasley-Murray, Paul
  Dynamic leadership.
  1. Christian life. Leadership
  I. Title
  248.4

ISBN 1–85424–073–0

Printed in Great Britain for
MARC, an imprint of Monarch Publications Ltd
1 St Anne's Road, Eastbourne, E Sussex BN21 3UN by
Courier International Ltd, Tiptree, Essex
Typeset by J&L Composition Ltd, Filey, North Yorkshire

To Caroline

Contents

1 Churches Need More Leaders   9
2 Leadership the Jesus Way   21
3 Leadership in Action: Working with Others   43
4 Leadership in Action: Defining the Task   55
5 Leadership in Action: Achieving the Task   79
6 Leadership in Action: The Team   93
7 Leadership in Action: Teams Within the Team   115
8 Leadership in Action: The Team Members   143
9 The Leader: Qualities for Leadership   177
10 The Leader: The Vital Relationship   197

Acknowledgements

I am grateful to Spurgeon's College for giving me a sabbatical in which to complete this work. I am also deeply appreciative of the work that my secretary, Mrs Audrey Jones, undertook in ensuring that this manuscript reached the publishers.

I

Churches Need More Leaders

1. Pastors are called to lead

Leadership is the key priority in the churches of today. Preaching is important, worship is important, pastoral care, evangelism and social action — all these things must come high on the agenda. But uppermost comes leadership.

It has been said,

> 'There are three requirements for a good programme within the church. The first is leadership, the second is leadership, and the third is leadership.' A lack of leadership may be part of the reason that in a typical year, an average of at least eight protestant congregations disappear every day. ... Churches need more leaders, not more members.[1]

These words were written of the American situation. But if they were true of churches on the other side of the Atlantic, they are even more true of churches in this country. Churches are dying for lack of leadership. Alternatively, many churches experiencing new life in the Spirit are being split asunder for lack of leadership.

It is because of this need for leadership that at Spurgeon's College we have developed our SALT programme: Spurgeon's Adaptable Leadership Training. This is the acronym which we have chosen to serve as the umbrella under which all our courses are structured. As a Baptist theological college, Spurgeon's is in the business of training up leaders for today's and tomorrow's churches. Such leadership training is not intended to demote the study of theology. We have not turned our backs on academic theology. Rather, we are seeking to make theology the servant of the church. The church of God needs not so much mini-theologians as leaders who can think theologically. Leadership — and leadership training — is the name of the game.

Pastors are called to be leaders. They are called to be leaders in the sense that they are called to lead the flock of God. Indeed, the very metaphor 'pastor', which is derived from the Latin word for a shepherd, suggests leadership. As the shepherd goes ahead and leads his flock, so too the pastor should go ahead and lead God's people. It is interesting to note that the church was not the first group of people to use this particular metaphor to describe leadership. In the ancient world generally the term 'shepherd' was used as a title for kings and rulers.

Pastors are not the only leaders in the church. Indeed, later on we shall argue that every church should enjoy the benefits of a plurality of leadership. Pastors are called to share the leadership of the church with their elders and/or deacons or whatever their leadership structure is called. Not to do so is to grieve the Holy Spirit by denying the use of those leadership gifts given by the Spirit to others in the fellowship. Yet, for all the importance of shared leadership, it remains true to say that pastors are called by God to spearhead the life and work of the church. They are called to be the leaders of the leaders and, together with them, to help give direction and purpose to the life of the church.

This emphasis on the role of the pastor as leader is still relatively new. It is an emphasis which emerged only during the 1970s. Before then the term 'leader' was hardly used in many churches. Indeed, it is only fairly recently that leadership training has arrived on the curricula of our theological colleges.

In his book *What on Earth Is this Kingdom?* (Kingsway: Eastbourne 1983), Gerald Coates, the house–church leader, caricatures the life of many a Baptist church when he writes, 'Resist the devil and he will flee from you — resist the deacons and they will fly at you.' And yet, for all the caricature, there is an element of truth in his facetiousness. There have been times when deacons were a negative force to be reckoned with. Not for nothing, some pastors used to say, that the generic term for a group of deacons was a 'gloom' of deacons! One pastor even remarked, 'Deacons can make Herod look compassionate!' But today, more often than not, deacons can be viewed as a much more positive force, anxious to encourage their pastors to give a lead, and then to follow. Certainly I can do nothing other than pay tribute to the splendid deacons with whom I have had the privilege to work in the past. In a very real sense they made my ministry — not least by encouraging me in my leadership.

An interesting comment on life as it was among the Free churches is provided by Michael Saward, the Vicar of Ealing. Writing as an Anglican he says:

> Free or Independent churches tend to reduce the position of the minister ... to that of one who fulfils their wishes. It takes a very fine church (or an especially able minister) to avoid that trap, which may be why relatively few major exciting reforms seem to have come out of the British nonconformist tradition in recent years.[2]

These are sobering words. There is little doubt that Michael Saward's comments are an accurate reflection of how life has been for many pastors in the past. In too many churches the pastor has been regarded as the paid servant of the church, there to fulfil every whim of the congregation.

2. 'Pastor, you should be the spark plug!'

Today the scene is changing, if not changed. The importance of pastoral leadership is increasingly recognised. In part, at least, this may be due to the contribution of the church growth movement, which has stressed the important role of strong pastoral leadership. Thus, according to Peter Wagner, 'strong pastoral leadership' is the first vital sign of a healthy, growing church. He further interprets this sign in terms of 'a pastor who is a possibility thinker and whose dynamic leadership has been used to catalyse the entire church into action for growth'. Somewhat provocatively — at least as far as the British scene is concerned — he goes on to say, 'Pastor, you should be the spark plug! ... Pastor, don't be afraid of your power!'[3]

In one of his later books, *Leading Your Church to Growth*, Peter Wagner continues to emphasise this point:

> The important factor that determines church growth or decline is its leadership. From Guatemala, Mardoqueo Munoz says, 'The role of the pastor is exceedingly crucial in the life of the church.' Gordon Moyes, pastor of Australia's largest church, Wesley Central Mission in Sydney, affirms that 'the minister is the key person in a growing church ... All growing churches have a strong ministry'.[4]

This view of the pastor as 'the primary catalytic factor for growth' was confirmed by Alan Wilkinson and me in our study of 350 English Baptist churches (see *Turning the Tide* (Bible Society: London, 1981), pages 31–37). In other words, this is no mere Californian phenomenon. We established, for instance, that leadership, vision and possibility thinking all represent key gifts of a pastor in a growing church. Strange as it may sound, even the gifts of preaching and pastoral care are less significant for growth than the gifts of administration and leadership/vision.

All this is no new insight. In 1976 Ted Engstrom made the same point: 'The successful organization has one major attribute that sets it apart from unsuccessful organizations: dynamic and effective leadership.'[5] What is true of organisations generally is also true of churches. More recently, Eddie Gibbs has again emphasised the importance of good pastoral leadership:

> To face an aggressively secular society the Church of Jesus Christ urgently needs leaders who are prepared to serve more in the style of the commando than the caretaker. It is a high risk, all-or-nothing challenge. . . . The major obstacles to Church Growth lie largely with the churches — not within the populations that they have been divinely commissioned to reach.[6]

Alas, in the past, leadership has not been taken seriously. Henry Ford once wryly made the remark that he took the church's survival as a sign of God's existence. No other enterprise run so poorly could stay in business! Happily the picture is changing. The importance of leadership is being recognised. Increasingly leadership is now seen as a priority. It is to this theme that this book is devoted.

3. What is leadership?

So far we have been talking about leadership. But what do we mean by this term? What is leadership?

Andrew Le Peau, in his book *Paths of Leadership*, quotes a number of great leaders of the past. Harry Truman, for instance, once said, 'A leader is a person who has the ability to get others to do what they don't want to do, and to like it.' That sounds like manipulation! Mahatma Ghandi identified tenacity as the key element: 'To put up with misrepresentation and to stick to one's guns come what may — this is the essence of leadership.' Hannibal, as he contemplated crossing the Alps, typified this attitude: 'I will find a way or make one.' Other definitions include Napoleon, who believed 'a leader is a dealer in hope'. Or the ancient Chinese philosopher, Lao-tse, who once said, 'A leader is best when people barely know he exists.' All fascinating insights into leadership. Andrew Le Peau himself defines leadership as 'any influence any person has on an individual or group to meet its needs or goals for the glory of God'.[7]

To these definitions one could add a whole number more. Lord Montgomery, for instance, defined leadership as 'the capacity to rally men and women to a common purpose, and the character which inspires confidence'.[8] Ted Engstrom writes: 'When God creates a leader, He gives him the capacity to make things happen.'[9] He quotes Nicholas Murray Butler, a former President of Columbia University: 'There are three kinds of people in the world — those who don't know what's happening, those who watch what's happening, and those who make things happen,' and adds:

> Though leadership may be hard to define, the one characteristic common to all leaders is the ability to make things happen — to act in order to help others work in an environment within which each individual serving under him finds himself encouraged and stimulated to a point where he is helped to realize his fullest potential to contribute meaningfully.[10]

John Haggai advocates WCH Prentice's definition of leadership: 'Leadership is the discipline of deliberately exerting special influence within a group to move it toward goals of beneficial permanence that fulfil the group's real needs.'[11]

My own preferred definition is that advocated by John Adair who writes of the good leader as one who 'works as a senior partner with other members to achieve the task, build the team, and meet individual needs'.[12] It is this definition with which we shall work throughout the rest of this book.

4. Three circles form the key

To illustrate the relation of these three functions — achieving the task, building the team, and meeting individual needs

— Adair develops a three circles model often used in group dynamics courses:

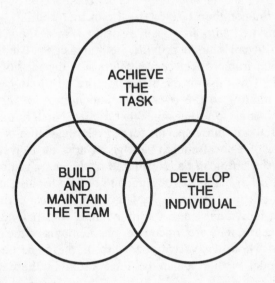

He comments:

The three circles-diagram suggests that the task, group and individual needs are always interacting upon each other. The circles overlap but they do not always sit on top of each other. In other words, there is always some degree of tension between them. Many of an individual's needs — such as the need to achieve and the social need for human companionship — are met in part by participating in working groups. But he can also run the danger of being exploited in the interests of the task and dominated by the group in ways that trespass upon his personal freedom and integrity.[13]

Adair goes on to argue that each of the circles must be seen in relation to the other two. Thus, if a group fails in its task, this will intensify the disintegrative tendencies present in the group and diminish the satisfaction of individual needs. If there is a lack of unity or harmonious relationships in the group, this will affect performance on the job and also individual needs. If an individual feels frustrated and unhappy, he will not make his maximum contribution to either the common task or the life of the group.

Translated into language associated with the Christian church, Adair's model provides helpful insights. Clearly, in a Christian frame of reference, the task is the mission of the church. This mission might be interpreted in large general terms relating to the overall implementation of the Great Commission. On the other hand, the mission might be interpreted in more specific terms, relating to the particular mission of a local church in a given area at a given time. Again the term can be interpreted of the church in general. On the other hand, there is much to be said for also applying it to the leadership team serving within a local church. As for the individuals, and the individuals who belong to the senior team, they are, of course, the members of the church, each of whom has varying needs to be met. The beauty of the model is that it can be interpreted in these various ways.

The model also draws out helpfully the need for balance. There are, for instance, some churches which are so task-orientated (whether it be evangelism or social action) that the needs of the church, as also the needs of members, are neglected. Again, there are churches which are so concerned to meet the needs of the team (through, for instance, an over-emphasis on small groups: in church growth jargon, 'fellowshipitis in extremis'), that the needs of the wider world are forgotten. Or again, there are some churches which are individual-orientated: teaching is the be-all-and-end-all — mission and fellowship are neglected. There is a need for balance. Leaders should always be aware of both the group and the individual, see to their needs, and yet at the same time ensure that they are harmonised in the service of the common task. Leadership in these terms is very much a balancing act! Yet, on reflection, to use such language is not helpful. Balance implies maintenance: whereas if the task of the church is not to be forgotten, direction is necessary too.

5. Leaders do not just manage

How does leadership relate to management? Are leaders managers? The answer is that leaders may often be good managers, but good managers are not necessarily good leaders. Leadership involves motivating others into action. Once motivation is supplied, management then gets to work to ensure that the mission is fulfilled. Lord Slim defined the relationship between leadership and management thus: 'Leadership is of the spirit, compounded of personality and vision; its practice is an art. Management is of the mind, more a method of accurate calculation, of statistics, of methods, of timetables and routines; its practice is a science. Managers are necessary; leaders are essential.'

The distinction between the two is drawn out in Ted Engstrom's eight points (adapting distinctions first made by Olan Hendrix):

(1) Leadership is a quality;
   management is a science and an art.
(2) Leadership provides vision;
   management supplies realistic perspectives.
(3) Leadership deals with concepts;
   management relates to functions.
(4) Leadership exercises faith;
   management has to do with fact.
(5) Leadership seeks for effectiveness;
   management strives for efficiency.
(6) Leadership is an influence for a good among potential resources;
   management is the co-ordination of available resources organized for maximum accomplishment.
(7) Leadership provides direction;
   management is concerned about control.
(8) Leadership thrives on finding opportunity;
   management succeeds on accomplishment.[14]

Peter Wagner puts it even more simply: 'Leadership captures concepts, vision and overall direction. Once those are established, management sees that it is done. . . . Leadership decides where we are going and why. Management figures out how to get there.'[15] He then goes on to identify leadership and management with the spiritual gifts of 'leadership' (Rom 12:8) and 'administration' (1 Cor 12:28).

I am not convinced that in Romans 12 and 1 Corinthians 12 Paul was actually making a distinction between leadership and management. As we shall see in the next chapter, Paul had something else in mind. Nonetheless, the general point Wagner is making is fair enough. Certainly his observations of pastoral life today are helpful:

> Few pastors are pure leaders or pure administrators. Most are a mix of the two. But I have observed that pastors who tend toward being leaders, whether or not they also are administrators, will most likely be church growth pastors. Pastors who see themselves to be administrators and use that kind of management style tend to be maintenance orientated. Making sure that the church as it is functions smoothly and harmoniously is usually where a manager is. A leader, on the other hand, is willing to take risks and upset the status quo in order to move out towards new horizons.[16]

In conclusion leadership cannot be equated with management pure and simple. Whereas management is intent on oiling the works and keeping the plant going, leadership gives direction and purpose. People follow leaders — they do not follow managers.

Notes

1. Lloyd Perry, *Getting the Church on Target* (Moody Press: Chicago, Il, 1977), p 73.
2. Michael Saward, *All Change* (Hodder and Stoughton: London, 1983), p 30.

3. Peter Wagner, *Your Church Can Grow* (Regal Books: Glendale, CA, 1976), pp 55–68.

4. Peter Wagner, *Leading Your Church to Growth* (Regal Books: Ventura, CA, 1984), p 127.

5. Ted Engstrom, *The Making of a Christian Leader* (Zondervan: Grand Rapids, MI, 1976), p 11.

6. Eddie Gibbs, *Followed or Pushed?* (MARC: Bromley, 1987), pp 10–11.

7. Andrew Le Peau, *Paths of Leadership* (Scripture Union: London, 1984), pp 9–10.

8. Quoted in Michael Saward, *op cit*, p 34.

9. Ted Engstrom, *op cit*, p 19.

10. *Ibid*, p 20.

11. John Haggai, *Lead On* (Word: Waco, TX, 1986), p 4.

12. John Adair, *Effective Leadership* (Pan Business/Management: London, 1983), p 51.

13. *Ibid*, p 38.

14. Ted Engstrom, *op cit*, p 23.

15. Peter Wagner, *op cit*, p 87 f.

16. *Ibid*, p 89.

2

Leadership the Jesus Way

1. A gift to exercise

Leadership is a gift

All God's people are called to serve, but not all are called to lead. Indeed, not all are gifted to lead. As Paul so delightfully makes clear in 1 Corinthians 12, God gives many and various gifts. 'If they were all one part, where would the body be? As it is, there are many parts, but one body' (1 Cor 12:19, 20).

A secular illustration of this truth — leadership is a gift given only to some — was illustrated in an article in *The Observer* a number of years ago. Colin Wilson set out to show that only some 5% of people have leadership qualities. He wrote:

> One of the most closely guarded secrets of the Korean war was why there were no escapes of American prisoners. The Chinese wanted to economise on manpower. So instead of keeping all the prisoners under heavy guard, they watched them for a day or two, and picked out all the 'leader' figures: anyone who seemed to have imagination or enterprise. These were guarded heavily. The rest were left with almost no guard at all. And without the leaders no one tried to escape.

The 'dominant' types, the Chinese found, were always pre-cisely 5% of the total number of soldiers. The same figure also applies to animals. In experiments concerned with the effect of overcrowding among rats, Dr John B Calhoun of the U.S. National Institute of Mental Health, discovered that the 'domi-nant' rats numbered 5% of the total.[1]

Hence the title 'One rat in twenty is a leader'. If this figure is applied to the church, then perhaps we would only expect there to be five leaders among any 100 church members! True, we are talking here of leadership in natural terms, but time and again spiritual gifts are but natural gifts dedicated to the service of the Lord.

A gift of the Spirit

It is significant that 'leadership' is to be found in all three lists of spiritual gifts in Paul's writings. True, the actual term 'leadership' does not always appear in our English trans-lations, but the idea is most certainly present.

Romans 12

Leadership is one of the seven gifts itemised in Romans 12:6–8. Thus in Romans 12:8 Paul writes, 'If it is leadership, let him govern diligently.' A similar translation is offered by the New English Bible: 'If you are a leader, exert yourself to lead,' and also by the Good News Bible: 'Whoever has authority should work hard.' On the other hand the Revised Standard Version translates this same phrase: 'He who gives aid, with zeal.' How can this be?

This confusing state of affairs is brought about by the fact that the underlying Greek verb could mean both 'to lead' and 'to care for'. Theoretically, therefore, both the trans-lations offered by the NIV and the RSV are equally possible. However, probably, at the end of the day we should not seek to distinguish too clearly between these two meanings. The two meanings interrelate. Here indeed is a helpful hint of what pastoral leadership is all about. Pastoral leadership is not about the exercise of power, but rather about the exercise of care. Interestingly, Michael Green notes that at one stage the noun derived from the verb used in Romans 12:8 originally denoted the powerful Roman 'patron' who had 'clients'. The word then came to be applied to any person of wealth and influence, who used his position to benefit the less fortunate. It was, for instance, this word which was applied to Phoebe in Romans 16:2: 'She has been a great help to many people, including me.' Michael Green rightly comments: 'The word sheds a fine light on the nature of Christian leadership.' The Christian leader is the one who uses his influence for the good of others.[2]

1 Corinthians 12

Turning to the list of gifts of the Spirit in 1 Corinthians 12, we find a reference to 'those with gifts of administration' (1 Cor 12:28) — or at least, that is how the Greek is translated by the NIV. The RSV adopts a similar translation: it talks of 'administrators'. Perhaps it is not surprising, in the light of these translations, that in many a talk on Christian stewardship this gift has been interpreted as belonging to a person gifted as a 'secretary' — i.e. one who is able to offer help in some of the essential administrative tasks of the church.

Such exegesis is misleading. Almost certainly this gift refers to an aspect of leadership. Thus the GNB translates, 'those who are given power to direct'. Similarly the NEB talks of those who have 'power to guide'. The fact is that the underlying Greek noun literally means 'helmsmanship'. It was a term often used metaphorically in Greek literature of the art of government: the statesman guiding the 'ship of state'. Here, of course, the ship in question is the church. The leader is the one who keeps his hand on the tiller, who ensures that the ship is kept on course.

The Anglo-Catholic John Gunstone has some perceptive comments to make on this metaphor:

The leader of the (charismatic) prayer meeting is the man at the helm. The gathering is driven along by the wind of the Spirit, but unless the leader's hand is firmly on the tiller, there is every danger that the ship's course may be deflected by the cross-currents of human emotions and ambitions that move not very far below the surface of the sea over which she sails.[3]

Gunstone later goes on to argue that this gift is basic to a pastor's ministry.

Through a deeper appreciation of the concept of an every-member-ministry, the spiritual gift of the ordained minister is seen to be that of 'presidency' (i.e. 'helmsmanship'). He is not the one who has every spiritual gift necessary for the congregation, nor is he necessarily a specialist in some of the functions that are normally attributed to him (e.g. teaching or counselling). But what he has above all is the charisma of leadership which enables him to preside over a congregation in its worship, life and mission, in such a way that he enables individuals and groups in that congregation to minister with the gifts that God gives them.[4]

Gunstone goes on to comment that a ship with no one at the helm is a frightening place to be!

These comments of Gunstone are refreshingly helpful. Every pastor needs the gift of 'helmsmanship'. Only in that way can they lead. Indeed, without that gift it may be questioned whether a pastor has the right to be a pastor. However, this does not mean that pastors do not need other gifts. We shall see that pastors need teaching gifts — while counselling gifts are an added bonus!

Ephesians 4

In Ephesians 4:7–13, the ascended Christ is said to give gifts to his church. Unlike the gifts in Romans 12 and 1 Corinthians 12, these gifts are seen primarily in terms of 'office' rather than 'activity': 'It was he who gave some to be apostles, some to be prophets, some to be evangelists, and some to be pastors and teachers' (Eph 4:11).

This verse is often wrongly seen as listing five separate offices or ministries in the church: apostles, prophets, evangelists, pastors and teachers. In fact, the underlying Greek makes it clear that Paul is not speaking of five different offices or ministries, but four. Thus only one definite article covers both 'pastors and teachers'. In other words, when the risen Christ gave gifts, he gave apostles, prophets, evangelists and pastor-teachers.

The main point, however, that needs to be made at this stage of the argument, is that the office of leadership, present in the ministry of the pastor-teacher (and presumably present too in the ministry of an apostle) is a gift. There is no room for human pride. All is of God!

A gift for women too

Women are clearly gifted, but are they gifted to lead? This has been — and still is — a burning issue in some circles. The clear, biblical answer is: yes! The hierarchies of Jew over against Gentile, of slave over against free, of male over against female, no longer exist in Christ (Gal 3:28). In Christ a revolution has taken place. The old order has passed, a new order has come! Women can and should expect to play varying roles within Christian leadership.

Romans 16 is a crucial text in this regard. For as a careful examination of the chapter makes clear, women played a key role in the first-century church. Paul names a whole succession of women: Phoebe, Priscilla (or Prisca), Mary, Junia, Tryphena and Tryphona, Persis, the mother of Rufus, Julia, and the sister of Nereus. All these women had made a singular contribution to church life. What is more, the contribution of at least three of these women had been in the area of leadership.

Phoebe (Rom 16:1–2), for instance, was a 'deacon' (not 'deaconness' as the NIV renders; in the Greek New Testament there is no separate female order of deacons). Clearly she was a woman of some influence. Paul in fact uses of her a word used of the senior partner in the patron-client relationship of Roman society.

Priscilla (Prisca) (Rom 16:3; also Acts 18:18, 26, and 2 Tim 4:19) is mentioned before her husband Aquila. The implication is that she took the lead in church life, not least in the teaching of Apollos (Acts 18:26).

Junia (Rom 16:7), most interestingly of all, is described with her husband (?) Andronicus as 'outstanding among the apostles'. Modern New Testament scholarship rightly argues that Junia (*not* Junias, as the NIV wrongly renders; 'Junias' is the accusative form of Junia) was a woman.

CEB Cranfield comments:

> That Paul should not only include a woman ... among the apostles but actually describe her, together with Andronicus, as outstanding among them, is highly significant evidence ... of the falsity of the widespread and stubbornly persistent notion that Paul had a low view of women and something to which the Church as a whole has not yet paid sufficient attention.[5]

What then of the passages most frequently quoted in defence of all-male leadership (1 Cor 11:3–16; 14:33–36; 1 Tim 2:11–15)? How are they to be understood? Without going into the argument in detail, it would appear that these passages are culturally bound. Certainly, on hermeneutical grounds, if 1 Corinthians 11 rules out women's leadership today, then consistency demands that women do not cut their hair and wear veils for worship. You cannot have the one without the other. There is no middle ground!

The Scriptures teach that the Spirit gives his gifts irrespective of gender (Acts 2:17–18). Leadership cannot be restricted to men. Throughout this book, therefore, any reference to leadership always envisages both men and women.

A gift to be developed

If leadership is a gift, then such a gift has to be developed and trained. Just as a preaching gift is no excuse for not learning how to preach (hence the institution of sermon class in our theological colleges!), so a leadership gift is no excuse for not learning how to lead.

It is at this point that we enter the debate of whether leaders are born or made. My own conviction is that leaders are both born and made. In the words of Bennie Goodwin, a black American educationalist: 'Although potential leaders are born, effective leaders are made.'[6] Leadership is without doubt a gift — a 'charisma'. But if that gift is to be used, then it needs to be trained.

Furthermore, such training involves study, and not just experience on the field. Thus Lord Montgomery, who believed that leaders are made and not born, told of how, during the First World War, he suggested to an officer that he ought to go to one of the junior staff college courses which were held in France:

> He ridiculed my suggestion, saying that the thing which really counted in war was practical experience in the trenches. I then told him of Frederick the Great's remark about officers who relied only on their practical experience and who neglected to study — that he had in his army two mules which had been through forty campaigns, but were still mules.
>
> 'No officer,' said Montgomery, 'will reach the highest rank without study.'[7]

The implications for Christian leadership are surely clear. 'God's gifts have to be cultivated and leadership potential has to be developed.'[8] It is to this task that theological colleges seek to devote themselves. No theological college can 'make' a pastor. It is God who calls and God who gifts. But colleges can develop gifts God has given and thus enable students to become what God intended them to be. On reflection, is this not what education generally is about? Does not the very word 'education' (from the Latin *educere*: to draw out) imply the drawing out and developing of talents both latent and potential? Theological training is not a luxury, it is a necessity. Indeed, training courses of every kind are to be welcomed in the pursuit of developing the leadership gifts God has given his church.

Let the leaders lead

It is not sufficient to be gifted, nor indeed to be trained in the exercise of whatever gifts one is given. Gifts are to be used. Leaders are to lead. In the words of Paul: 'Having gifts that differ according to the grace given to us, let us use them' (Rom 12:6, RSV).

There is no room for false modesty. The cause of Christ is not furthered if people hide their 'lights' under a 'bushel'. Nor for that matter is there room for timidity. Of course, it's much more comfortable being just one of the 'boys' — the moment you raise your head above the parapet, you become the target for the snipers. For that reason some have abrogated their call to leadership. It's not worth the pain and the risk!

Siegfried Sassoon tells the lovely story of the army padre who, seeing off young soldiers as they left for the Somme, enthused: 'God will go with you to the trenches, and I will go with you to the railway station.'[9] But if you are a leader, then your task is to go out with the troops and lead them into battle. There is all the difference in the world between being a chaplain and being a leader. Pastors are not called to a life of comfort and security — they are called to leadership!

Needless to say, leaders are called to lead for the benefit of others. As with any other spiritual gift, the gift of leadership is to be used for the good of others. As Paul puts it in 1 Corinthians 12:7: 'to each the manifestation of the Spirit is given for the common good'. In the body of Christ there should be no such thing as an ego-trip!

2. A service to render

Leadership gifts are to be exercised. This is the clear teaching of the New Testament. But there is a very necessary proviso: leadership gifts are to be exercised in the spirit of Jesus the Servant. Pastoral leadership is servant ministry. This too is the clear teaching of the New Testament.

The teaching of Jesus

On a number of occasions Jesus emphasised the necessity of the servant role if a person would be a leader. Thus, when James and John asked if they might sit at his right and left hand in glory, Jesus replies: 'You know that those who are regarded as rulers of the Gentiles lord it over them, and their high officials exercise authority over them. Not so with you. Instead, whoever wants to become great among you must be your servant, and whoever wants to be first must be slave of all' (Mk 10:42–44; Mt 20:25–27; see also Lk 22:24–26).

Leon Morris makes the telling comment: 'Jesus is not saying that if his followers are to rise to great heights in the church they must first prove themselves in a lowly place. He is saying that faithful service in a lowly place is itself true greatness.'[10] This comment simply echoes the words of the great Manchester New Testament scholar, TW Manson: 'In the Kingdom of God service is not a stepping-stone to nobility: it is nobility, the only kind of nobility that is recognized.'[11]

Clearly such teaching about servant ministry must have been a constant theme of Jesus. Thus on another occasion when his disciples were arguing as to who was the greatest, Jesus said: 'If anyone wants to be first, he must be the very last, and the servant of all' (Mk 9:35; Lk 9:48). Matthew 23 is a salutary chapter for any leader to read, for there Jesus denounces the Pharisees and the other religious leaders of his day. He condemns those who 'love the place of honour', who 'love to have men call them "Rabbi"'. 'The greatest among you will be your servant.' There is no room for pride in the heart of the Christian leader.

Jesus not only taught servant ministry, he lived out the life of a servant. Nowhere do we see this more clearly than in his action in the upper room. John describes the scene. Jesus, who 'knew that the Father had put all things under his power ... wrapped a towel round his waist ... and began to wash his disciples' feet' (Jn 13:3–5). When he had finished, he said, 'I have set you an example that you should do as I have done for you' (Jn 13:15). We are so familiar with this incident that perhaps we do not always sense the degradation of the scene. Within the context of his Jewish culture, Jesus humiliated himself beyond measure as he served his disciples by washing their feet.

> The menial nature of footwashing in Jewish eyes is seen in its inclusion among works which Jewish slaves should not be required to do ...; the task was reserved for Gentile slaves and for wives and children. ... The action of Jesus in removing his outer garment and tying a towel around him underscores the humiliation of his action; the Midrash on Gen 21:14 states that when Abraham sent Hagar away he gave her a bill of divorce and took her shawl and girded it around her loins, that people should know that she was a slave.[12]

Jesus the Servant took upon himself the role of a slave as he washed his disciples' feet. Today's leaders would do well to heed his words: 'I have set you an example that you should do as I have done for you' (Jn 13:15).

The teaching of the Apostles

The teaching of Jesus was taken up by the apostles. Paul, for instance, was very clear that he was a 'servant of Christ Jesus' (eg: Rom 1:1; Phil 1:1) and so in turn a 'servant' of the church: 'I have become its servant by the commission God gave me to present the word of God in its fulness.' Paul would not yield an inch to the 'false apostles' of Corinth, yet at the same time, while knowing himself to be a true apostle, he had no false illusions of grandeur for himself. 'What, after all, is Apollos? And what is Paul? Only servants through whom you came to believe.' John Stott makes the helpful comment:

The excessive and misguided loyalty which they were giving to certain leaders was due to their false view of ministry. . . . It is to be noted that he does not even ask, 'Who is Apollos? Who is Paul?' He is determined to speak of himself and Apollos disdainfully, almost disrespectfully. So he uses the neuter; as much as to say, 'What on earth do you think we are, that you should attach such importance to us?'[13]

In the light of all this it is not surprising that in 2 Corinthians 4:5 Paul later writes: 'We do not preach ourselves, but Jesus Christ as Lord, and ourselves as your servants for Jesus' sake.'

From Paul we turn to Peter. Peter too stresses the servant role of the leader. Thus to the elders of the churches he writes: 'Be shepherds of God's flock that is under your care, serving as overseers — not because you must, but because you are willing, as God wants you to be; not greedy for money, but eager to serve, not lording it over those entrusted to you, but being examples to the flock' (1 Pet 5:2–3). Here surely is a clear allusion to Jesus' teaching in Mark 10:42. Leaders are not to lord it over their people. There is no place for autocratic behaviour in the church. Instead, says Peter, 'clothe yourselves with humility towards one another' (1 Pet 5:5). Here Peter is almost certainly alluding to the foot-washing incident of John 13: in clothing themselves with humility, leaders should imitate their Lord, who tied a towel about himself in order to wash his disciples' feet.

Leaders still do well to heed Peter's exhortation. For as one commentator rightly says:

How extensively does the worldly view of power penetrate and permeate the life of the Church! The truth of the saying that 'power corrupts' is far too often confirmed in the Church, and when spiritual leadership is abused in this way, 'the corruption of the best is the worst'. Again, the danger is all the more formidable, because we are all good at self-deceit.[14]

A reversal of values

This emphasis on servant ministry was revolutionary as far as the first-century society was concerned. Service was not a commonly admired virtue. Thus Herman Beyer wrote of the prevailing Greek attitude of that day:

> In Greek eyes serving is not very dignified. Ruling and not serving is proper to man. ... The formula of the sophist: 'How can a man be happy when he has to serve someone?' expresses the basic Greek attitude. ... For the Greek, the goal of human life is the perfect development of an individual personality. ... Logically, the sophist argues, a real man should simply serve his own desires with boldness and cleverness.[15]

Nor was the Jewish attitude of that day much better. Beyer notes that service had become a method of gaining merit for oneself. Furthermore, such service was not to be accorded to the unworthy!

It was in this context that Jesus reversed all human ideas of greatness and rank. He reversed all human ideas not just in what he said, but how he lived. For he, the Lord of glory, emptied himself of all that was rightfully his and took the form of a servant (Phil 2:6). In so doing he offered a model not just to Christians in general, but to leaders in particular. It was in this light that Bernard of Clairvaux wrote: 'Learn the lesson that if you are to do the work of a prophet, what you need is not a sceptre but a hoe'!

How do things stand in our twentieth-century society? Thanks to the influence of Christian thinking and teaching down through the centuries, things have changed. Today service is a virtue that is admired. We do admire the Mother Teresas of this world who give themselves in the service of others. But do we emulate them? The fact is that the old Adam is still rampant. The 'natural' tendency is still to pursue the interest of self. Servant ministry — even in the church — is 'unnatural'. For it threatens to dethrone self. But the way of Jesus is the way of the servant. Only that leadership which patterns itself on the Servant-King can truly call itself Christian.

Leadership is service

This teaching on the importance of servant-leadership must not, however, lead us to underplay the importance of leadership itself. Leadership, rightly understood, does not stand in opposition to service. Rather leadership can be an expression of service. If leadership is undertaken for the sake of others, rather than for the sake of one's own personal ego, then such leadership is service in the cause of Christ.

Indeed, leaders do the Lord and his church a disservice if they do not exercise their gifts and offer leadership. Where would the church of God be without its leaders? As Richard Foster rightly points out: 'An infantile anarchy in church life is no better than oppressive dictatorship.'[16] In the words of Chrysostom, 'Anarchy is an evil, the occasion of many calamities, and the source of disorder and confusion.' Leadership in itself is good. Indeed, leadership is necessary. The church needs the service of its leaders. It is only the exercise of 'worldly' leadership which is to be rejected. This tension — between the desirability of leadership and the danger of 'worldly' leadership — is well expressed by CK Barrett: 'A church that rejects the gifts of leadership will greatly impoverish itself; a church that allows them to develop in a worldly way will destroy itself.'[17]

The key to Christian leadership is servant-leadership. Servant-leadership focuses on the people to be cared for rather than just the job to be done. There is therefore a very real difference between the servant-leader and the high-powered executive. The servant-leader cannot trample on people in the pursuit of personal advancement. Indeed, the servant-leader cannot trample on people even in pursuit of the kingdom. Leaders may not be doormats — but neither may they use others as doormats!

Servant-leadership is non-coercive

It is precisely because Christian leadership is servant-leadership, that we may go on to say that pastoral leadership may never be coercive: ie, it can never force another to do something over which they are basically unhappy. In this context the words of 1 Peter 5:2–3 are again relevant: leaders are not to 'lord it over those in their charge'. Alas, in the context of this century, the term 'leader' conjures up autocratic associations. Thus Adolf Hitler called himself *der Fuehrer*, the leader; and similarly Benito Mussolini called himself *il duce*, the leader. The Nazi dictator and the Fascist head of state exercised autocratic powers. But this is not the way of Christian leadership.

There is a difference between 'leadership' and 'lordship'. Leadership may be authoritative, but it may never be authoritarian. Peter Wagner tries to spell out the difference in the following way:

The difference often depends on the focus of power. When the pastor realizes he is an under-shepherd, receiving his authority from the Word of God, he gives an authoritative leadership to his church. When the pastor localizes power in his personality, he gives authoritarian leadership to the church.[18]

Alas, it is all too easy to confuse the two. It is all too easy to deceive oneself.

Perhaps the difference between leadership and lordship is seen best of all in the difference between leading sheep and driving sheep. Thus the Chinese leader, Chua Wee Hian, commenting on our Lord's words in John 10:3b–4, tells the lovely story of how an Arab guide was once showing a group of tourists around the Holy Land.

On one of their coach trips he alluded to the tradition of the Palestinian shepherd walking in front of his flock. While he was speaking, the tourists spotted a man in the distance driving a small flock of sheep with a rather menacing stick. Just as all school children love to prove their teachers wrong, they pointed the figure out to the guide. He immediately stopped the bus and rushed off across the field. A few minutes later he returned, his face beaming. He announced, 'I have just spoken to the man. Ladies and gentlemen, he is not the shepherd. He is in fact the butcher!'[19]

The good shepherd leads his flock. Leading does not involve driving. Pastoral leadership is always a servant ministry which leaves people free to accept or not to accept its direction. This point needs to be emphasised today, since in recent years some leaders in the Restoration movement, in reaction to the lax discipline present in most mainline churches, have tended to become unduly authoritarian in their leadership. Thus, in an early membership handbook emanating from the Harvestime group of churches (*Belonging to an Anointed Body*, p 20), submission to the leaders of the church was put on the same level as submission to God. By paralleling Hebrews 13:17 ('Obey your leaders and submit to their authority') with James 4:7 ('Submit yourselves . . . to God') the impression was given that there was little difference between 'obedience' to the elders and 'submission' to God. But there is a difference. Men are fallible, God is infallible.

But to return to Hebrews 13:17: surely the injunction to 'obey your leaders' implies that leaders have authority? Of this, of course, there is no question. Leaders do have authority. But this does not mean that their authority may not be questioned. The underlying Greek verb which the author uses does not imply unthinking obedience; rather, as Philip King has pointed out, it has 'the meaning of being persuaded by, or being convinced by someone, and suggests reasoned exhortation rather than authoritarian command'.[20] Indeed, the root meaning of the verb is 'to persuade'.

Leadership may be authoritative. It may not be authoritarian. It is interesting to examine Paul's understanding of authority in 1 Timothy. In a situation in which false teaching was being spread, Paul was conscious of the need for strong action to be taken, action ultimately based on his apostolic authority (1 Tim 1:1). Paul therefore commands (1 Tim 1:18; 6:13–14) Timothy to take action by in turn commanding wayward church members to fall into line (1 Tim 1:3, 5; 4:11; 5:7). However, the word that is used is an interesting one: military in origin, it has the meaning of 'coming alongside to pass on a message'. It is not the shout of command of a regimental sergeant-major drilling his men on the parade ground. Clearly Paul expected Timothy to take a strong line — and yet not to act as a mini-dictator. 'Do not rebuke an older man harshly, but exhort him as if he were your father' (1 Tim 5:1). This is pastoral leadership, rather than authoritarian leadership. Pastoral leadership which does not coerce, but rather exhorts.

Servant-leadership can never be from 'above', it must always be from 'below'. This is brought out by Paul in 1 Corinthians 16:15–16: 'The household of Stephanas ... have devoted themselves to the service of the saints. I urge you, brothers, to submit to such as these and to everyone who joins in the work, and labours at it.' Submission goes hand in hand with service. As David Prior comments: 'Christian submission is not a duty to be imposed but an attitude which is spontaneously undertaken in response to sacrificial love.'[21] John Goldingay makes a similar point: 'The authority of leaders is not based on their position in a structure but on the fact [if it be fact] that they embody true Christian living [ie, service] and bring the true Christian message, which will be known by its content and not merely by its origin.'[22] Or to put it even more simply: it is as leaders begin to win the trust of their people by the kind of people they in turn are, that authority is gained. Ultimately people obey their leaders not because of what they say but because of who they are!

3. A task to share

Leadership is a gift to exercise, a service to render. It is also a task to share. The 'monarchical episcopate' enjoyed by so many Baptist churches and other independent evangelical churches receives no justification in Scripture. The New Testament knows nothing of a one-man ministry. In the New Testament church there was always a plurality of leadership. Indeed, according to Colin Brown, 'It would seem to be the case, that if there was to be a church at all in the New Testament, it needed at least two ministers.'[23] Not without justification, therefore, Andrew Le Peau writes: 'Organisations that are built on the preaching, teaching, thinking, entertaining, fund-raising charisma of one person — of which there are many in Christendom — are built contrary to Scripture. These are not bodies. These are grotesque mutations.'[24]

Plurality of leadership in the New Testament

The evidence for the plurality of leadership in the New Testament is as follows:

Jesus sent his disciples out in twos. Mark writes that on one occasion Jesus sent the Twelve out 'two by two' (Mk 6:7). Similarly, Luke in his account of the mission of the Seventy (or Seventy-two), speaks of the disciples being sent out 'two by two' (Lk 10:1).

Why were the disciples sent out in twos? What was to be gained by being together? In some ways it might be argued that more people might have heard the Good News if the disciples had gone out one by one. The German New Testament scholar, Joachim Jeremias, brings out the significance of what was in fact a Jewish custom (ie, not something just peculiar to Jesus):

It had a twofold significance: first, it was to protect the messengers; on lonely and dangerous roads it is good for the messenger to have someone at his side. On the other hand, sending out messengers in pairs was an application of the legal clause of Deuteronomy 17:6; 19:15, which originally applied to judicial proceedings: only statements on which two witnesses agree are trustworthy. In the same way, the one of the two who is the spokesman (cf Acts 14:12) is to have his yoke-fellow by him to confirm his message.[25]

In other words, the purpose of the pairing was more than simply providing mutual comfort and help — it underlines the validity of the message being proclaimed. However, as far as the disciples of Jesus were concerned, it surely also came to symbolise the fact that 'service for Jesus ... can never be done by only one person. The teamwork of at least two is a symbol of this truth.'[26]

The Apostles went out in twos.   In Acts 15:36–40, Paul and Barnabas separated from one another, but both took a travelling companion with them for their missionary journey: Barnabas took Mark, and Paul took Silas. The same pattern is evidenced on all of Paul's missionary journeys. Paul never worked alone.

The apostolic churches always had more than one leader. Thus Acts 13:1 implies that the leadership of the church at Antioch was in the hands of a group of 'prophets and teachers'. The leadership team there was composed of five men: Barnabas, Simeon called Niger, Lucius of Cyrene, Manaen and Saul.

In Acts 14:23 we read that in Asia Minor Paul and Barnabas 'appointed elders ... in each church'. The local church leadership consisted of a plurality of leaders.

In Acts 15:23 Luke tells us that the leadership of the Jerusalem church was made up of 'apostles and elders'. James was obviously the leader, but he did not lead on his own.

Likewise in Acts 20:17, 28, it is evident that the church at

Ephesus was not led by one man, but by a group of 'elders' (v 17) who are later described as 'overseers' or 'bishops' (v 28).

According to Philippians 1:1, the church at Philippi had 'overseers/bishops' (NB, plural!) and 'deacons' — not one minister and twelve deacons.

In the New Testament elders are always mentioned in the plural in each local church. The only exceptions to this are the two references to the qualifications of a bishop-elder in 1 Timothy 3:2 and Titus 1:7, but neither of these imply the existence of a single leader in a church. They are examples of what is known as a 'generic singular' (see 1 Tim 5:4–10 where the 'generic singular' is also used of widows).

Diotrephes — a warning rather than an example. The only example of a one-man ministry or leadership in the New Testament is perhaps to be found in 3 John 9 where 'the elder' writes of 'Diotrephes, who loves to be first'. However, as the letter clearly indicates, Diotrephes sets no example. 'He assumed a position of leadership in his congregation because of an egocentric lust for power, which he confused with zeal for the Gospel.'[27] CH Dodd makes the interesting comment that Diotrephes is in fact 'a symptom of the disease which the quasi-apostolic ministry of monarchical bishops was designed to receive'![28]

From this survey of New Testament evidence regarding the plurality of leadership, we may conclude with John Goldingay, 'For all the diversity of patterns in the New Testament, there is no example of the concentration of local leadership in one man.'[29] Leadership is always plural. Leadership is always corporate.

Shared leadership is advantageous

Corporate leadership in the church is not only scriptural. It also has great advantages over against the one-man model of ministry.

(a) Leaders are able to supplement one another, for no

one leader has all the gifts necessary for an all-round ministry. Members of a leadership team can build up one another's strengths and compensate for one another's weaknesses.

(b) Leaders are able to encourage one another. Leadership can be a lonely business, but where leadership is shared, there support can be derived. Members of a leadership team can identify one another's gifts and encourage each other to develop and use them.

(c) Leaders are able to be accountable to one another. It is not good either for the individual or the local church if a leader is not in a position to receive correction when things go wrong. Members of a leadership team should be able to speak the truth in love to one another, and so learn from failure and be the stronger for the future.

Presidency not ruled out!

Leadership is a task to be shared. This is the burden of this section. However, shared or corporate leadership does not rule out 'presidency'. A leader of the leaders is called for and will always emerge, whether or not it is formally recognised. Thus we have already seen that in Jerusalem, James was the presiding elder.

The question arises: who, within the context of the local church, should be the leader of leaders? Interestingly in German Baptist churches the 'church leader' (*Gemeindeleiter*) is never the pastor, but rather the person whom we would call the church secretary. My understanding of this custom is that it is relatively recent and in part a reaction to the Third Reich — too much power should not be put in the hands of one man. Certainly it is a custom which creates tensions — between pastor and church leader.

My own conviction is that pastors are called to be the 'senior partners'. Called to lead with others, they nonetheless are called to be the leaders of leaders.

Notes

1. Colin Wilson, 'One rat in twenty is a leader', *The Observer*.
2. Michael Green, *Freed to Serve* (Hodder and Stoughton: London, 1983), p 46.
3. John Gunstone, *A People for this Praise* (Hodder and Stoughton: London, 1978), p 39.
4. *Ibid*, p 69.
5. CEB Cranfield, *Romans II* (T and T Clark: Edinburgh, 1979), p 789.
6. Quoted by John Stott in *Issues Facing Christians Today* (Marshalls: Basingstoke, 1984), p 327.
7. Lord Montgomery *The History of Warfare* (Collins: London, 1968).
8. John Stott, *op cit*, p 238.
9. Quoted by Michael Saward, *All Change* (Hodder and Stoughton: London, 1983), p 20.
10. Leon Morris, *Tyndale New Testament Commentaries: Luke* (InterVarsity Press: Leicester, 1974), p 368.
11. TW Manson, *The Church's Ministry* (Hodder and Stoughton: London, 1948), p 27.
12. GR Beasley-Murray, *John* (Word: Waco, TX, 1987), p 233.
13. John Stott, *The Preacher's Portrait* (Eerdmans: Grand Rapids, MI, 1986), p 102.
14. CEB Cranfield, *1 and 2 Peter, Jude* (SCM: London, 1960), p 130.
15. Herman Beyer, quoted in Gerhard Kittel, ed, *Theological Dictionary of the New Testament II* (Eerdmans: Grand Rapids, MI, 1964–1974), p 82.
16. Richard Foster, *Money, Sex and Power* (Hodder and Stoughton: London, 1985), p 235.
17. CK Barrett, *Church, Ministry and Sacraments in the New Testament* (Paternoster: Exeter, 1985), p 40.
18. Peter Wagner, *Leading Your Church to Growth* (Regal Books: Ventura, CA, 1984), p 115–116.
19. Chua Wee Hian, *Learning to Lead* (InterVarsity Press: Leicester, 1987), p 35.
20. Philip King, *Leadership Explosion* (Hodder and Stoughton: London, 1987), p 133.
21. David Prior, *Bedrock* (Hodder and Stoughton: London, 1985), p 119.

22. John Goldingay, *Authority and Ministry* (Grove Booklets: Bramcote, Notts, 1976), p 23.

23. Colin Brown, 'New Testament Patterns of Ministry', in Clive Porterhouse, ed, *Ministry in the Seventies* (Falcon: London, 1970), p 19.

24. Andrew Le Peau, *Paths of Leadership* (Scripture Union: London, 1984), p 60.

25. Joachim Jeremias, *New Testament Theology I* (SCM: London, 1971), p 235.

26. Edward Schweizer, *The Good News According to Mark* (SPCK: London, 1971), p 129.

27. Stephen Smalley, *1, 2, 3, John* (Word: Waco, TX, 1984), p 356.

28. CH Dodd, *The Johannine Epistles* (Hodder and Stoughton: London, 1946), p 164.

29. John Goldingay, *op cit*, p 23–24.

3
Leadership in Action: Working with Others

The good leader, we have argued, 'works as senior partner with others to achieve the task, build the team, and meet individual needs'. Leadership, according to this definition, involves working with others. Time and time again this theme surfaces in this book. It may be self-evident to many. Nonetheless, in view of the ubiquity of one-man ministries up and down the country, it only seems right and proper to highlight this crucial understanding of pastoral leadership.

1. All God's people are called to ministry

Pastoral ministry is shared ministry, because all God's people are called to ministry. Because of this, it is unhelpful to call pastors 'ministers' as if ministry can be limited to one particular group of people in the church. Rather all God's people are ministers. As one church notice-board expressed it:

Pastor: Jo Bloggs
Ministers: All of us

My own view is that the custom of some 'ministers' wearing dog-collars and dressing up differently from their fellow

church-members is unhelpful. It simply reinforces the popular view that somehow they are different from other people
— different not just in function but also different in kind. By
wearing distinctive 'ministerial' garb they have opted out of
the human race!

In the light of this fact, in the preamble to an ordination
service I always state:

> .... [name] is not called to serve God on his/her own. For God
> has gifted all his people with many varied gifts for service. If the
> ministry of .... [name] is to be effective, it will be to the degree
> that he/she is willing to enable God's people to fulfil their
> particular ministries.

Traditionally, Protestants have prided themselves on their
doctrine of 'the priesthood of all believers'. But by and
large they have failed to draw out the implications of this
Reformation slogan, with the result that it has made very
little difference to the way in which they have lived their life
together. Thus Howard Snyder observes: 'For the most part
... this doctrine has been understood soteriologically rather
than ecclesiologically. That is, it has been understood to
mean that all Christians have direct access to God without
the mediation of a human priest.'[1] The doctrine has been
interpreted vertically, in a God-ward fashion, rather than
horizontally, in a man-ward fashion. But to be a priest is also
to represent God to others — it is to build a bridge (the Latin
for priest, *pontifex*, actually means 'bridge-builder') between
God and others.

To be fair, certain ecclesiological implications of this doctrine have been drawn, but all too often in a very restricted
sense. Thus in popular Baptist thought the priesthood of all
believers has amounted to little more than two things: any
Christian may 'preside' at the Lord's Table; any church
member has as much right to be heard at the church meeting
as the pastor. These two things are true. But the emphasis is
unhelpful: it emphasises 'rights' rather than responsibilities.

Surely a more helpful and challenging slogan is that of 'the ministry of all believers'. Here responsibilities come very much to the fore. This doctrine is founded on such texts as Ephesians 4:11–12: 'It was he who gave some to be apostles, some to be prophets, some to be evangelists, and some to be pastors and teachers, to prepare God's people for works of service,' or as the RSV puts it, 'to equip the saints for the work of ministry'. Here, the ministry that Paul has in mind above all is the ministry of the whole people of God. Much mischief, alas, was done by the old Authorised Version, which punctuated these verses in such a way that a comma came between 'saints' and the rest of the sentence ('For the perfecting of the saints, for the work of ministry, for the edifying of the body of Christ'). Such punctuation was entirely misleading: the body can in fact only be built up as Christians are 'prepared' or 'equipped' for the work of the 'ministry'. The church, it has been rightly said, is not only a 'universal priesthood'; it is also a 'universal diaconate, for all God's people are called to *diakonia*', ie, to service.[2]

The Anglican, John Tiller, suggested that there should be 'a "*ministry roll*" in each local church of all those who are prepared to express their baptismal commitment in an appropriate context ... [for] through baptism they have already received all the authorisation that is necessary for them to act as lay ministers of Christ'.[3] Tiller, it seems, is belatedly suggesting that Anglicans adopt the Baptist pattern of linking baptism to church membership. However, before Baptists begin to smile smugly, they should ask themselves: does their theory of church membership work out in practice? Is church membership understood above all as commitment to service?

In this connection it is interesting to note that many Baptist churches are reviving the old practice, once common among them, of the 'laying-on of hands' immediately after baptism. Here prayer is made that the baptismal candidates be filled afresh with the Spirit of God and thus empowered for service (see Acts 1:8). Or, as the Baptist worship manual

Praise God (Baptist Union: London 1980, p 140) puts it: 'Bless, O Lord, this your servant. Strengthen him [her] by the Holy Spirit, as we now in your name commission him [her] for the service and ministry of Jesus Christ our Lord.' Surely this is a form of ordination? For here the newly baptised are 'ordained' for Christian service.

2. All God's people are gifted for ministry

Let's continue to remind ourselves of the obvious. All God's people are gifted for service. Thus Paul writes in Ephesians 4:7 (GNB) — 'Each one of us has received a special gift in proportion to what Christ has given.' Likewise, we find in 1 Corinthians 12:11 (GNB) — 'The Spirit gives to each one, just as he determines.' Anybody who is Christ's has received the Spirit, and in receiving the Spirit has received some kind of spiritual gift. Nobody is called to be 'pew fodder', for spiritual gifts are for all. In a very real sense, all Christians are 'charismatic'. Unfortunately, all too often it has only been the 'charismatics' who have taken the gifts seriously.

Furthermore, spiritual gifts are given not to wallow in, but rather to be used in God's service. 'Now to each one the manifestation of the Spirit is given *for the common good*' (1 Cor 12:7, GNB, my italics). Gifts are not given to be treasured, but rather to be exercised in the service of others.

Indeed, if the gifts of the Spirit are not used correctly, then Christ is frustrated in his purpose of building up his body, the church. This seems to be the implication of Ephesians 4:11–12 — 'He gave some to be apostles [etc] . . . to prepare God's people for service.' It has often been pointed out that the word Paul uses here for 'preparing' (NIV) or 'equipping' (RSV) was in the context of surgery applied to the setting of broken bones. May we therefore say that where Christians are not using their gifts, there the church can be likened to a hopeless cripple? Furthermore, in the context of fishing, this word could be used of the mending of nets (see Mt 4:21). May we therefore say that where Christians are not fulfilling their ministries, then there the church will have as much success in winning people for Christ as a fisherman seeking to catch fish with gaping holes in his net?

Whatever, the clear implication is that every Christian has a part to play if the body is to function properly. Conversely, where only one member — the pastor — is playing a part, then there the body is suffering from what Michael Green once amusingly described as 'elephantisis': 'some member, usually the minister, has grown to a size far greater than he ought to do. The result is that other parts are inhibited from making their contribution and so he finds himself doing all sorts of tasks for which he is not fitted.'[4] The body has become a monstrosity!

All God's people are called and gifted for ministry. Together they are called to 'faithfully [administer] God's grace in its various forms', or, more literally, they are called to be 'stewards of God's many-coloured grace' (1 Pet 4:10–11). Howard Snyder helpfully comments:

> The pure light of God's manifold grace is ... refracted as it shines through the Church, as a light through a prism, producing the varied, multi-coloured *charismata* or gifts of the Spirit. The Greek word *poikilos* in 1 Peter 4:10 and Ephesians 3:10 often expresses the idea of 'many-coloured', as in the variety of colours in flowers or clothing. This suggests that the pure, intense but invisible light of God's glorious grace is made colourfully visible in the diversity of spiritual gifts in the Christian community.[5]

What a delightful picture!

3. Pastoral ministry is specialised ministry

It is only within the context of every-member ministry that one can talk of the particular ministry of the pastor. This, of course, then raises the question: what is the specialised ministry a pastor is called to exercise? Clearly, as the title of this book implies, leadership is a key role. But what else is involved in pastoral ministry?

The Bible Society, in its church growth courses, has a thought-provoking exercise in which participants are asked to list in order of priority their perception of a pastor's tasks. In all there are fourteen different tasks.

(1) *Visiting.* Calling on members of the congregation in their homes. Door-to-door visitation in the neighbourhood. Factory or prison visits.

(2) *Teaching.* Expounding the Scriptures and relating them to the contemporary world and daily life.

(3) *Counselling.* Counselling individuals on personal and spiritual problems.

(4) *Administration.* Serving as 'managing director' of the congregation; working with planning and finance committees.

(5) *Evangelism.* Calling on the uncommitted people in the community. . . . Preaching evangelistic sermons.

(6) *Team Leadership.* Serving with the lay leadership team.

(7) *Training.* . . . Training leaders to teach groups, perform counselling and visiting functions and engage in evangelism.

(8) *Community Leadership.* Involvement in secular community organizations.

(9) *Congregation Leadership.* Serving as *the* . . . person to whom members turn for advice and guidance on all aspects of the life and work of the congregation.

(10) *Personal Development and In-service Training.* Developing devotional life, and pastoral, teaching and management skills.

(11) *Denominational and Ecumenical Responsibilities.*

(12) *Leading Worship.* . . . Conducting public worship and working with others who participate in leading corporate worship.

(13) *Enabling.* Helping others identify their own special call to service and ministry.

(14) *Sacramental and Priestly Functions.* Ministering the sacraments. . . . Conducting marriages and funerals. Spending time in prayer for and on behalf of the congregation and the community.

What a list! What an exercise! If this exercise were conducted at a deacons' meeting, then clearly much fruitful discussion would result. Hopefully it would be readily perceived that the pastor cannot be the general factotum.

But can't the list of responsibilities be simplified? I believe it can. Indeed, at an ordination service I generally list six particular roles of a pastor.

Within this general context of shared ministry .... [name] is called to fulfil a number of particular roles.

First and foremost, ... is called to be a man/woman of God. If a pastor is to lead the flock, he/she first needs to be led.

Secondly, ... is called to be a leader. Under God he/she is called to give a lead in worship, as in the general life of the church.

Thirdly, ... is called to be a teacher — the flock must be fed.

Fourthly, ... is called to exercise pastoral care — the flock must be tended.

Fifthly, ... is called to be an evangelist — the lost need to be sought.

Finally, ... is called to be an enabler — the people of God need to be prepared for Christian service.

Again, this list of specific responsibilities might appear to be all-embracing. However, none of these roles is exclusive to the pastor. Otherwise we would simply have one-man ministry through the back-door, as it were. All these responsibilities can be shared, but not all of them can be delegated. In the first instance, the call to be a man (woman) of God apart, the pastor is called to be a leader, a teacher and an enabler. These are roles which cannot be delegated. These are roles which dare not be neglected. Neither can pastoral care, evangelism and social action be neglected — but on the other hand, they can and should be delegated. This does not mean that pastors will not involve themselves in pastoral care, evangelism and social action. It does, however, mean that the burden of these important areas of

Christian service will be borne by others. Pastors have the responsibility to ensure that the pastoral care, evangelism and social action are carried out in and by the church. The more, however, that is shared by others, the better.

Interestingly Rowley Croucher comes to a similar conclusion. He lays down as one of his Ten Commandments for Pastors: 'Your tasks are only three — to pray, teach, and train/delegate (Exodus 18:13 ff; Acts 6:1–4).' He goes on to suggest that pastors spend their mornings with God, their afternoons (and about three evenings) with people (half people-time with leaders) and the rest (after a day(s) off) in administration.[6]

Pastoral ministry calls for balance. Some pastors get sucked up in administration. Thus according to Roy Oswald one survey revealed that the average pastor spends 33% of his time in administration, and effectively, in terms of time spent, this becomes his number one priority.[7] On the other hand, some pastors put too many eggs in the pastoral basket, and this is not helpful either, particularly when the task of pastoral care can be shared. Administration, provided that it is not simply shoving pieces of paper around, is important. Robin Greenwood is right when he says, 'I have found that to have the courage to put as a priest's primary role leadership of all the ministries around him, means taking administration seriously, constantly encouraging the work of teams, groups and committees.'[8] But this role should be balanced with the other key tasks of a pastor.

But to return to my general point: pastoral ministry is specialised ministry. The pastor is not called to be the Reverend Dogsbody. Pastors, like all God's people, have been called to a particular ministry.

4. Pastoral ministry demands inner security

If pastors are to work effectively with others, then they need to be secure in themselves. In particular, they must feel secure in their calling and gifting by God.

Experience, unfortunately, shows that insecurity is a great problem in pastoral ministry. 'Team ministry,' commented one perceptive associate pastor, 'can only really work where the senior pastor is well-integrated and secure in himself. Anyone who has doubts or is insecure becomes threatened or jealous and will threaten the growth and ministry of the associate.'[9] To this we would add: 'and threaten the growth and ministry of all who seek to work with him/her'.

There is no greater need than for pastoral ministry to be characterised by inner security. Would that all 'ministerial' selection committees examined more seriously the psychological make-up of prospective candidates. At Spurgeon's we have a detailed reference form for prospective 'ministerial' students which seeks to probe into the depths of people's personalities. Questions like the following appear:

How would you describe the applicant's self-confidence?

(a) lacking in self-confidence?
(b) over self-confident?
(c) naturally self-confident?

How does the applicant respond to criticism?

(a) accepts it and acts on it, if it is constructive?
(b) takes it, even if not constructive?
(c) reacts negatively against any form of criticism?
(d) sometimes misinterprets other comments as criticism?
(e) takes offence and reacts in an outgoing manner?
(f) takes offence and reacts by withdrawal into his/her self?

Pastoral ministry demands a sense of inner security. Otherwise there is no way in which pastors can work effectively with others.

5. Working with other 'professionals'

Increasingly as churches are growing they are employing extra members of staff. Instead of just the pastor, there is often a Senior Pastor and an Associate or Assistant. The question arises: at what point should a church consider increasing its full-time staff? According to Peter Wagner, 'Before the church slows down at the 200 barrier at least one more programme staff member should be on the board.'[10] However, David Womack makes the point: 'Most pastors hire assistant pastors much too soon. Until a church reaches 250–300 the church would do well to hire janitorial help to free the pastor from the physical upkeep of the church properties and competent secretarial help to support the pastor with an efficient office.'[11] Certainly, the importance of competent secretarial help cannot be overemphasised. If pastors are to be freed to fulfil their ministry, then they don't just need someone who can do a few letters for them now and again. They need a Personal Assistant. A competent PA is an absolute boon to any pastor.

Churches appointing multiple staff should, however, note that there is one great danger when extra full-time members of the pastoral staff are called: the new members of the pastoral team may actually stunt the ministry of the other members of the church. Lyle Schaller notes: 'One of the basic causes of passivity in many congregations is the "let's hire it in" syndrome.'[12] This 'hiring-it-in' syndrome in fact runs counter to the biblical pattern of every-member ministry. When new members of the pastoral staff are appointed, then churches should seek to ensure that as a result God's people are better equipped for their ministry, and not deprived of ministry.

6. The discipline of working with other 'professionals'

If pastors are to work effectively with their associates or assistants, then a certain 'discipline' of relationships needs to be maintained. This was one of the findings of a survey I made of team ministry in Baptist churches. Both senior pastors and associates/assistants were asked to share one tip on how to 'manage' an associate/assistant. Interestingly, the same points were made time and time again by both senior pastors and their associates:

Communication is vital. According to one associate, this is *the* potential weak area in team ministry. The senior pastor must keep his associate informed and vice versa.

Openness. 'Be open — share everything' was how one put it.

Trust your colleague. 'The senior minister must be willing to give up responsibility,' said one. 'Define areas of responsibility and give freedom within that responsibility', to which one associate added, 'Even if he does not do it your way.' Or as another put it, 'Let him do his own thing; what helped me at the beginning was the confidence the senior minister had in me.'

Accountability. Responsible delegation involves reporting back. Wrote one experienced pastor, 'If I was starting again I would want a greater degree of accountability.'

Respect. Typical comments included: 'Respect each other's calling, training, personality and gifts,' and, 'Learn how to use creatively the emerging gifts and talents of the associate.'

Self-awareness. 'Recognise both your weaknesses and limitations and also those of your colleague.'

Patience. 'Don't expect too high too soon — the relationship has to grow gradually.'

Encouragement came high. 'Encouragement is so important in the early years,' wrote one assistant. 'Constant reaffirming and appreciation' are needed.

Frankness is also valued. 'Be honest with gentleness' was one suggestion. An associate, not a senior pastor, wrote: 'Deal with problems as they emerge. Do not allow them to ferment. Today's niggle could be tomorrow's resentment, and next week's breakdown.'

Loyalty was also mentioned. 'Never let people play off one against the other,' said one. 'Do not publicly overrule any decisions he makes in his area of responsibility,' said an associate.

Good relationships are absolutely vital. 'Get to know them as persons and not just as colleagues'; 'Build a deep friendship'; 'It is vital the leaders are friends [inside and outside of work]'; 'Associate ministry stands or falls on the relationship present and evident between the senior and the associate'. One wise and experienced pastor likened the relationship between a senior pastor and his associate to a marriage: 'There is the senior partner who takes full responsibility. Within this relationship there is love, mutual trust, encouragement, and a determination to work harmoniously together.'[13]

If pastors are to work effectively with others — and in particular here with fellow 'professionals' — then they need to ensure that they discipline themselves to maintain a healthy relationship. Relationships don't always just happen. They have to be worked on.

Notes

1. Howard Snyder, *Liberating the Church* (Marshalls: Basingstoke, 1983), p 169.
2. John Stott, *One People* (Falcon: London, 1968), p 47.
3. John Tiller, *A Strategy for the Church's Ministry* (CIO Publishing: London, 1983), p 79.
4. Michael Green, *To Corinth with Love* (Hodder and Stoughton: London, 1982), pp 51–52.
5. Howard Snyder, *The Community of the King* (InterVarsity Press: Downers Grove, Il, 1977) pp 61–62.
6. Rowley Croucher, *Grid*, Spring 1988 (World Vision, Australia).
7. Roy Oswald, *Clergy Stress* (Alban Institute: Washington, 1982), p 102.
8. Robin Greenwood, *Reclaiming the Church* (Collins/Fount: London, 1988), p 74.
9. 'Dynamic Duos' in *Today* magazine (February 1989), p 11.
10. Peter Wagner, *Leading Your Church to Growth* (Regal Books: Ventura, CA, 1984), p 212.
11. David Womack, *The Pyramid Principle of Church Growth* (Bethany: Minneapolis, MS, 1977), p 86.
12. Lyle Schaller, *Activating the Passive Church* (Abingdon: Nashville, TN, 1981), p 47.
13. Paul Beasley-Murray, 'Dynamic Duos', *Today* magazine (February 1989), pp 7–11.

4
Leadership in Action: Defining the Task

The good leader, I have argued, works as a senior partner with other members to achieve the task, build the team and meet individual needs. The question arises: what is the task of the team? What is the mission of the church?

1. The Great Commission

In a previous book, *Turning the Tide* (Bible Society: London, 1981), Alan Wilkinson and I argued that making disciples is the fundamental task of the church. We took the words of Jesus in Matthew 28:18–20 as foundational:

> All authority in heaven and on earth has been given to me. Therefore go and make disciples of all nations, baptising them in the name of the Father and of the Son and of the Holy Spirit, and teaching them to obey everything I have commanded you. And surely I will be with you always, to the very end of the age.

The Duke of Wellington was right when he declared these words to be the marching orders of the church. Here is the 'Great Commission'. This is the task of the church.

Making disciples

Let's explore this Great Commission.

First of all, notice that 'making disciples' involves far more than winning men and women to Jesus Christ. It involves both 'baptising' and 'teaching'. Making disciples is a process. A disciple is not made when a person surrenders his or her life to Christ. Conversion is the essential beginning of the discipleship process, but it is just the beginning. Indeed, the new convert has yet to discover all that surrender to Christ truly involves.

Secondly, 'making disciples' involves the church. That, surely, is implicit in the reference to 'baptising'. For in New Testament terms at least, baptism is the moment of entry into the church. As Paul wrote to the church at Corinth: 'For we were all baptised by one Spirit into one body' (1 Cor 12:13). This emphasis on the church may sound strange to some Baptists — but that simply indicates how far some Baptists have departed from the New Testament! Ask the average Baptist the meaning of baptism and you would hear it primarily defined as an act of obedience or an act of confession. Baptism is, of course, these things too, but primarily it is an act of commitment — commitment to Jesus and his church. In baptism we identify with our Lord in the first place (Rom 6:3–4), but also with his people (1 Cor 12:13). Baptism, like the Lord's Supper, has corporate implications.

To the theologian there is nothing revolutionary about such an understanding of baptism. Yet if such thinking were adopted in all Baptist churches, then a revolution would have taken place. For although Baptists cannot be rivalled in their enthusiasm for evangelism on the one hand, and baptism on the other hand, many have yet to see the two as inextricably linked. Winning people for Jesus Christ is seen as separate from baptising people in the name of Christ. It is this which in part accounts for the strange phenomenon that in many Baptist churches baptism is an optional extra; ie, it is possible to become a member of a Baptist church without being baptised! It is this which also accounts for another equally strange phenomenon that in many Baptist churches church membership is an optional extra: ie, it is possible to be baptised without becoming a member of the local expression of the body of Christ. Alas Baptists, along with fellow evangelicals, have ceased to be true to their heritage and have developed an anaemic doctrine of the church. Perhaps a healthy dose of Catholicism would do them good! For Bishop Cyprian was right theologically when he stated, 'Outside the church there is no salvation!'

Body evangelism

But to return to the Great Commission. The implication is clear: Jesus calls his followers not to make converts, but to make disciples — disciples baptised into the body. This means therefore that evangelism which is true to its New Testament roots is evangelism which brings people into the body of Christ. The task of the church involves what has been termed 'body evangelism'.

Here we come across one of the positive emphases of the church growth movement. Evangelism which does not lead to incorporation into the church is both unbiblical and ineffective. It is like spending all one's effort in delivering a baby only to abandon it in the delivery room! When this kind of evangelism is practised on a large scale it leads to infant genocide. If this sounds a little dramatic, then an examination of para-church crusade evangelism proves to be a sobering exercise. Thus Win Arn, one of the pioneering American church growth leaders, once stated that statistics show a mortality rate of 75%: only one in four who profess a 'decision for Christ' actually make it to the point of church membership. In the world of medicine any practitioner guilty of such misconduct would be struck off the books. In the church we lay the blame on the hardness of people's hearts rather than on the conduct of the evangelist. How strange!

A learning curve

The discipleship process is not finished with baptism and church membership. The Great Commission sees the disciple-making process as involving 'teaching' too. There has to be a learning curve leading to maturity and service. The task of the church involves spiritual growth as well as numerical growth. We are to 'present everyone perfect [mature] in Christ' (Col 1:28; see Eph 4:15–16).

On the whole, most evangelical churches are good at Bible study. But does such Bible study produce the goods? Does it lead to maturity and service? If so, then why is it that so many churches are crying out for leaders? Why is it that such churches are apparently failing to develop their own people? How clearly has the task of spiritual formation been perceived?

A statement of mission

Every church needs to develop its own statement of mission in which it seeks to express its understanding of its task. As an example, let me give a statement of mission, based on the Great Commission of Matthew 28, which Alan Wilkinson and I produced in *Turning the Tide* (p 66). Deliberately simple in format — church people do not flourish on high-flown theology — it proved a helpful framework in which to exercise ministry at Altrincham Baptist Church. Let me reproduce it:

The mission of the church is:

— to do everything to God's glory and in accordance with his will as it is earnestly sought in prayer

— to bring men and women under the rule of Christ and into the committed membership of his church

— to nurture new Christians and also those older in their faith (though not necessarily in the same place and at the same time) so that all may share their faith, win others for Christ and his church, and demonstrate by their words and actions the love of God as shown in Jesus Christ.

This is to be done by:

(a)   The way believers live their lives, both as individuals and together with other Christians.

(b)   The way they share their lives in supporting and caring for one another and by responding to each other's joys and sorrows.

(c)   By the work they do in giving their time and financial resources for the good of the local church.

(d)   By the acts of social service they perform, not only for the fellowship but also in the community, both local and widespread.

(e)   By their teaching and pastoral care within the fellowship.

(f)   By their evangelism among those attending church and by going out into the neighbourhood.

(g)   By the quality of their worship.

2.   Lausanne bifocals

But is the Great Commission actually the Great Commission? Does Matthew 28:18–20 truly sum up the task of the church? In recent years evangelicals have developed a more holistic understanding of mission, with the result that social action has been twinned with evangelism.

This broader understanding of mission among evangelical Christians came to a particular focus at the International Congress on World Evangelisation held at Lausanne in 1974. It was out of this great congress that the Lausanne Covenant came, which affirmed that 'evangelism and socio-political involvement are both part of our Christian duty' (paragraph 5). True, 'in the church's mission of sacrificial service evangelism is primary' (paragraph 6), but such evangelism, it was recognised, must take place in the context of a 'deep and costly penetration of the world' (paragraph 6).

Since Lausanne there has been the International Consultation on the Relationship between Evangelism and Social Responsibility held at Grand Rapids, Michigan, in 1982, which in its report likened evangelism and 'social activity' to 'the two blades of a pair of scissors or the two wings of a bird'. Just as proclamation and service characterised the mission and ministry of Jesus, so they are to characterise ours (*Evangelism and Social Responsibility*, p 23).

The Grand Rapids Report (*Evangelism and Social Responsibility*, pp 43–46) went on to distinguish between different forms in which social concern should manifest itself:

Social Service	Social action
Relieving human need	Removing the causes of human need
Philanthropic activity	Political & economic activity
Seeking to minister to individuals & families	Seeking to transform the structures of society
Works of mercy	The quest for justice

The question was then raised: 'Does social action belong to the church as a church, or is it the prerogative of individual believers who make up the church, and of groups?' No agreed answer was forthcoming at that stage.

This, then, is the context in which evangelical thinking and action has been developing. Since Lausanne, increasingly social action, and not just social service, has been coming to the fore. Thus John Stott, in his report on NEAC 3 (the 1988 National Evangelical Anglican Celebration at Caister), wrote:

> It is generally accepted amongst us that 'mission' denotes everything Christ sends us into the world to do as his servants and witnesses. We are also clearer that 'compassionate service' cannot stop at philanthropy, but demands political action too in the quest for justice. For it is impossible to preach the gospel and ignore the social needs of those to whom we preach it.[1]

A sea-change has indeed taken place in evangelical thinking. Lausanne marks the turning-point.

Let us then return to the question with which we began: is the Great Commission actually the Great Commission? Does Matthew 28:18–20 truly sum up the task of the church?

John Stott has argued that, contrary to popular thought, Matthew 28 does not contain the Great Commission. Rather, the Great Commission is to be found in John 20: 'As the Father sent me, I am sending you' (Jn 20:21)

> Jesus sends us 'into the world' to identify with others as he identified with us ... to become vulnerable as he did. It is surely one of the most characteristic failures of us Christians, not least of us who are called evangelical Christians, that we seldom seem to take seriously this principle of the Incarnation. ... It comes more natural to us to shout the gospel at people from a distance than to involve ourselves deeply in their lives, to think ourselves into their culture and their problems, and to feel with them in their pains. Yet this implication of our Lord's example is inescapable. As the Lausanne Covenant put it: 'We affirm that Christ sends his redeemed people into the world as the Father sent him, and that this calls for a similar deep and costly penetration of the world' (para 6).[2]

Under the all-embracing term of 'mission', Stott would link 'The Great Commission' and 'The Great Commandment': 'Here then are two instructions of Jesus — a great commandment, "love your neighbour" and a great commission, "go and make disciples".'[3]

More recently, attention has been drawn to the 'Nazareth manifesto' of Luke 4:18–19 as describing, in part at least, the church's mission:

> The Spirit of the Lord is on me,
> because he has anointed me
> to preach good news to the poor.
> He has sent me to proclaim freedom for the prisoners
> and recovery of sight for the blind,
> to release the oppressed,
> to proclaim the year of the Lord's favour.

Evangelicals — especially those involved in urban mission — have linked together the Nazareth manifesto of Luke 4

with the Resurrection mandate of Matthew 28. Thus Colin
Marchant writes:

> Too often it has been an 'either ... or'; either social justice or
> personal conversion. The great need has been to hold both
> together. The two streams will then flow into the key model of 1
> Corinthians 12 – the Body of Christ uniting believers in a total
> ministry of directed love towards the world in its anguish and
> yearning.[4]

This broader understanding of mission among evangelicals
is surely to be welcomed. In many ways this new emphasis is
a reflection of our calling to be both light and salt in the
world (Mt 5:13–16). In the darkness of this world we are to
point to Jesus, the light of the world; indeed, we are to let his
light shine through us. But also in a world that is rotting and
decaying, we are to hold at bay putrefaction by getting
involved in the world's structures, actively pursuing peace
and justice in our society. The task of the church cannot be
restricted to evangelism. The world needs to be seen through
Lausanne bifocals!

Incarnational growth

However, the wearing of Lausanne bifocals does not necessarily mean that the Great Commission of Matthew 28 is no
longer to be taken as a summary of the church's task. A
broader understanding of the Great Commission is also
possible which includes the Lausanne emphases.

Thus the command to 'make disciples' is not fulfilled
simply by 'baptising' men and women and then 'teaching'
them. A third participle is present — in the Greek, at least:
'going' (more accurately: 'having gone' — a past participle is
used). It is as we 'go' that we begin to make disciples. Jesus
does not command his followers in the first instance to
'preach', but rather to 'go'. Although from the vantage point
of a New Testament scholar we may be guilty of reading a
truth not necessarily present in the text, it does not seem

contrary to the overall teaching of Jesus to argue that here we may see a reference to the living out of the gospel in the lives of God's people.

In church growth terms, we have here a reference to 'incarnational' growth. The gospel is 'fleshed out', is 'embodied' in the lives of God's people. As the South American theologian, Orlando Costas once helpfully put it:

> By incarnational growth is meant the degree of involvement of a community of faith in the life and problems of her social environment; ie, her participation in the afflictions of her world; her prophetic, intercessory and liberating action on behalf of the weak and destitute; the intensity of her preaching to the poor, the broken-hearted, the captives, the blind, and the oppressed.[5]

Incarnational growth is thus the manifesto of Luke 4 writ large! It is the costly, loving, self-giving involvement of the church with all levels of society. It is 'going' in Jesus' name to 'make disciples'.

Three-P evangelism?

Another way of looking at incarnational growth is to use the three-P model of evangelism, popularised by Peter Wagner. According to this model, evangelism involves:
— presence
— proclamation
— persuasion

For effective evangelism to take place it is not sufficient for the gospel to be proclaimed; people have to be persuaded of the truth as it is in Jesus. Indeed, even before we begin to proclaim the gospel, we must first live out the gospel. For it is only as others see Christ and his love present in us that they will begin to listen to our proclamation of the gospel.

Gospel proclamation in itself is insufficient. As William Booth, the founder of the Salvation Army, so rightly said, 'If you see a starving man, don't preach to him. First fill his belly, and then he may be disposed to listen.' Sadly, the church has not always listened to him. Thus a group of evangelicals living in South Africa have drawn up a statement in which they say, 'Our proclamation has been swallowed up by the cries of the poor and the oppressed that it is now even impossible to hold conventional evangelistic campaigns in this war situation. These voices have become so loud that it has now become impossible to hear the church preach' (*Evangelical Witness in South Africa: Evangelicals critique their own theology and practice* Paternoster: Exeter, 1986).

More people have indeed been driven from the church by the hardness and ugliness of so-called Christians than by all the doubts in the world. Likewise, in reverse, more people have been brought into the church by the kindness of real Christian love than by all the theological arguments of the world. My mind, for instance, goes to one friend whom I sought to win over to Christ through argument, but failed. Instead, he was won to Christ through reading Malcolm Muggeridge's account of Mother Teresa. The importance of demonstrating the love of Jesus is further evidenced by research in North America, which is said to show that 83% of those who join churches do so because of the influence of family, neighbours, friends or colleagues at work. Our lives do count as part of gospel proclamation.

I therefore find the three-P model of evangelism convincing. Yet, on reflection, I am not convinced that it is the best exposition of incarnational growth. It can be misleading. It can reinforce an unfortunate misunderstanding of what social action and service is all about. It can, that is to say, give the impression that Christian service and action is but a means to an end — winning people to Jesus Christ. They are all part of the 'softening-up' process. But this is far from the truth. Nobody worthy of the name Christian feeds the hungry as part of a strategy to win the world for Christ. We feed the hungry simply because they are hungry. True, as the three-P model of evangelism illustrates, the cup of water given in Christ's name can prove to be so winsome that it becomes a step in the conversion process. Hopefully much Christian service is attractive in nature. But it is not necessarily so.

3. A broader dream?

So far we have been seeking to look at the task of the church in terms of the Great Commission of Matthew 28 or through the eyes of the Lausanne Covenant. Maybe a different approach might be helpful. Let's try dreaming!

Dreaming, the Scriptures declare, is a mark of the new age of the Spirit. Thus Peter on the Day of Pentecost, quoting from the prophet Joel, proclaimed: 'In the last days, God says, I will pour out my Spirit on all people. Your sons and daughters will prophesy, your young men will see visions, your old men will dream dreams' (Acts 2:17).

Some years ago I decided to do some dreaming. I sought to open myself to God's Spirit by allowing him to fill my mind with a vision of his purpose for my church. The resulting 'dream' ensued, as I put pen to paper.

My dream.

I dream of a WORSHIPPING church:
where worship is exciting and invigorating
where people expect to encounter God
where Sunday is a day not to be missed
where celebration is a hallmark, and yet where awe and humility
    are to be found
where worship is structured and yet free and flowing
where the Lord's Supper is central
where children as well as adults sense the life of the Spirit.

I dream of a BIBLICAL church:
where the word of God is at the centre,
where the exposition of God's word holds the place of honour
where the whole counsel of God is preached
where people expect to hear God speaking to them
where study is combined with devotion

where a wide range of 'electives' is offered
where all are encouraged to keep on learning.

I dream of a PRAYING church:
where prayer is seen as a privilege rather than a duty
where people expect God to hear their prayers
where husbands and wives pray together
where families pray together
where church members pray with and for one another
where the leaders pray regularly together
where the services are prayed for, but also where the needs of
the world are not forgotten.

I dream of a SPIRIT-FILLED church:
where all are open to the Spirit
where people are constantly seeking to be filled with the Spirit
where people expect to see God at work
where people are unafraid to venture deeper in the spiritual life
where no one gift is undervalued or overvalued
where every member has a part to play, for every member has a
gift
where people feel free to express their love for one another and
the Lord.

I dream of a FAMILY church:
where all feel they belong
where all the members are drawn together in home groups
where all rejoice together and all suffer together
where family life is promoted
where the emotional and physical needs of singles are met
where the old feel wanted and loved
where the casualties of family life are made welcome.

I dream of an EVANGELISING church:
where new people are seen at every service
where people expect to see friends won for Christ
where every month people come to know the Lord Jesus
where 'evangelists' are regularly visiting the district
where young people are reaching out to their friends
where new Christians are encouraged to exploit their old network of friends
where small groups are used for evangelism.

I dream of a SERVING church:
where the members serve one another
where the practical resources of the fellowship are shared
where our love for one another spills out to the world outside
where members are involved in the community
where those involved in the community are supported by others
where the needs of the 'weak' receive priority
where God's love is seen in deed as well as in word.

I dream of a LIBERATED church:
liberated from tradition
liberated from self-centredness
liberated from duty
liberated from pressure of time
liberated to serve the world
liberated to serve one another
liberated to serve God.

Phew! What a dream! Whether or not this is a valid approach to defining the task of the church may be questioned. Strictly speaking, the dream is not a definition, it is rather a description of an ideal church — a worshipping, biblical, praying, Spirit-filled, family, evangelising, serving and liberated church. It is a dream to live by and to work towards.

4. Direction needed!

However the task of the church is defined, it needs to be defined if the church is to have any hope of achieving its task. It needs in the first place to be defined by the leader — otherwise the leader is like the blind leading the blind. Alas, this picture all too often corresponds to reality. There are far too many church leaders who have no real sense of direction to their work — they are unsure of the task God would have them and their churches achieve. Their diaries — and the diaries of their churches — are packed full of activities. But activities to what purpose? Such churches are like a football team engaged in a 'game' on a field without goalposts. The players are content to kick and pass the ball, but no one tries to score. Or, to use a different analogy, some churches are spiritual Winnie-the-Poohs, not really knowing what they are 'hunting':

'Hallo!' said Piglet, 'what are you doing?'
'Hunting,' said Pooh.
'Hunting what?!'
'Tracking something,' said Winnie-the-Pooh very mysteriously.
'Tracking what?' said Piglet coming closer.
'That's just what I ask myself. I ask myself, "what?"'
'What do you think you'll answer?'
'I shall have to wait until I catch up with it,' said Winnie-the-Pooh.[6]

Some churches have no sense of direction. Other churches are torn in all kinds of directions. For there are competing interest groups present, with competing tasks. The result is disaster. Far from pulling together, the church is torn asunder. Or at the very best it stands still — for the sails are set in every direction. In such a context leadership is needed. Leadership which enables the church to define its task. For 'where there is no [united] vision, the people perish' (Prov 29:18, Authorised Version — adapted!).

Formulating goals

An overall philosophy of ministry is necessary — for pastor and people alike. However, no church thrives on philosophy. A broad definition of the church's task is helpful only to a degree. At some stage a wise leader will seek not only to define general objectives ('the task'), but also to formulate specific concrete goals for the immediate present. Churches need to know not only the general direction, but also the way that leads in that direction. If this is 'the task', then this is what we must do to achieve that task, and further, this is how we may set about doing it. In other words, goals need to be formulated.

But first, a rigorous assessment of the church needs to be

made. Otherwise any goals that may be set may not be meaningful and relevant. The question needs to be asked: in the light of the overall task that is ours, how does our church's performance measure up? How faithful are we? How successful are we? Not 'successful' in general terms, but in terms of the task.

Wise leaders will not just seek to make an assessment on their own. They will want to involve others. Indeed, the more others are involved in this particular exercise, the more the ultimate goals that are formulated are likely to be 'owned' by the church. How easy it is for leaders to draw up goals for the church — and then for the church to go on its way, heedless, regardless.

Surveying the church

One simple exercise for pastors to do with their deacons or equivalent leaders is to ask them to fill in a simple survey sheet, containing just four questions:

Survey Sheet:
(1) In three or four sentences describe your hopes for our church. What would you like to see this church become and do in the next few years?
(2) List five strengths of our church.
(3) List any weaknesses you see in our church.
(4) What needs and opportunities do you see as the top priorities for our church in the next year?

Ideally this survey sheet should be circulated in good time to all deacons, who should then return their responses to the pastor a week before their next meeting. This would then enable the pastor to correlate the responses and to suggest a way forward.

'Swotting'

A slightly different approach to goal formulation is the so-called SWOT analysis.[7]

S — strengths
W — weaknesses
O — opportunities
T — threats.

Here the intention is to identify the elements of the church on which to build (strengths), on which it would be unwise to depend (weaknesses), the areas ripe for development (opportunities), and those which it is as well to avoid for the time being (threats).

No doubt this can be a helpful analytical tool at certain stages of a church's life. However, as it stands there is no reference to the overall task of the church. Goals are best formulated within an overall objective.

5. Goal-setting is an art!

If a church is to be helped rather than hindered in its task, then care needs to be taken in the formulation of its goals. It may, for instance, be true that the task of the church is to win men and women for Jesus Christ and his church, but it is unhelpful for a small church of twenty-five members to then set themselves a goal of adding 250 new members to their church in the next twelve months. Such a goal immediately becomes irrelevant, because it is unachievable. It is tantamount to asking a deaf-mute to sing Grand Opera. It cannot be done.

There are, in fact, a number of simple rules for goal-setting.

Goals need to be achievable

We have already alluded to this simple rule. Eddie Gibbs tells the delightful story of how during the First World War, Will Rogers, a celebrated American raconteur, volunteered an idea for ridding the Atlantic Ocean of German U-boats. His novel answer to the problem was to bring the oceans to boiling point, so that all the U-boats would be forced to surface before their crews were pressure-cooked. Then waiting patrol-boats could force them to surrender. However, when Rogers was asked how he would go about heating the ocean, he replied, 'Oh, I'm just the ideas man. You work out the details!'

Such an approach to goal-setting is impossible. For a goal to be helpful, it must be achievable: it must be within reach of the people. True, it must not be so easy as to require no faith. The attempting great things for God must be balanced by the expecting of great things from God. Faith is a great catalyst for the Spirit of God. But faith must not be allowed to dissipate into foolish wishful thinking.

Goals need to be short-term

No doubt there is a place for long-range planning (it is said that anything over five years is a long-term goal), but such planning is dependent upon such a series of unknown factors that for the most part it is highly speculative if not fanciful. Certainly, if long-term goals are adopted, then they should be broken down into a series of short steps. These steps should take the form of annual goals.

Goals should be 'written in pencil'

If one week can seem to be a long time in politics, even more so is one year in the life of a church. Precisely because circumstances can change, goals need to be open to constant re-examination. It has been said that 'a goal is not a tyrant, but a target'. It is something to aim at, and not be bound by. A church should always have the freedom to say, 'We got it wrong.' It needs to have the freedom to redefine its goals — even within a twelve-month period.

Goals, incidentally, need not always be changed for negative reasons. I remember one occasion when we revised our budget upwards mid-term. We discovered that we had not exercised sufficient faith in our original budget-setting exercise, with the result that far more money was coming in than originally anticipated. Would that such budget (goal) revisions were more frequent in the life of our churches!

Goals should be measurable

It is only when goals are expressed in measurable terms that we can truly assess whether or not we have been successful. Thus it is not sufficient to say that we want to make more disciples next year. This is too generalised. A more specific target is called for. Thus a church may in faith set a target of ten people to be baptised in the coming year — they set a arget in that they believe God for it and work for it! Measuring spiritual growth is more difficult: the target here may simply be the running of an additional Bible-study group.

Goals should be evaluated

It is no use setting goals if we do not evaluate them at the end of the year or whatever the time limit may be. The results of our activity should always be assessed.

This, of course, can be an uncomfortable exercise. It may mean facing up to the fact that we have failed to achieve what we set out to achieve. Thus instead of seeing twenty people won to Christ through a mission, only two were won. But it is only by facing up to our failures that we can learn from them and make progress. It may be that the goal in the first place was unrealistic — maybe it was too much to expect twenty people to be won through a low-key mission. Alternatively, it may well be that we failed to implement the policies needed to achieve that goal: the mission itself went well, but the preparation was poorly done.

Whatever, we need to learn from our mistakes. In so doing we may comfort ourselves with the words of Spurgeon: 'The man who never made a mistake, never achieved anything.' As it is, all too often we draw a bull's-eye around the arrow and kid ourselves that we were successful, when in fact we were not!

Goals should be personal

Goals should be personal in the sense that they are personal to the church, and not just to the leader. Goals need to be owned by everybody, otherwise they come to nothing. It is no good pastors seeking to impose their own goals on the church without any discussion. Goals need to be talked through, to be accepted by everybody. Only then will people set to and work to implement them. This I have learnt through bitter experience.

6. Goal-setting is a process

I cannot overstress the fact that defining the task and thereafter formulating the goals is a *process* involving the whole church. Woe betide leaders who seek to hand their goals down to the church as Moses handed down the Ten Commandments to the people of Israel. There will be even more murmurings, and the goals deemed necessary by the leader will never be owned by the people.

The goal-setting process has three stages.

It begins with a dream

If a church is to go in the direction God wants it to go, then its leaders must take time to 'dream dreams' and 'see visions'. Leaders must take time to open their minds to God and think his thoughts after him.

For this to happen, time is of the essence. Time needs to be taken to discern God's will. With Mary, leaders need to take time to sit at Jesus' feet. As it is, they tend to identify with overactive Martha. They run like scalded bunnies from the beginning of one week to another, with scarcely a thought in between.

I have already suggested that pastors set aside a morning with their deacons to work out the church's priorities. However, the process of making time to 'dream dreams' should have begun before. Pastors, as the 'senior partner', should have set aside time to think and pray. Indeed, by their very office, they have been set aside to devote themselves to 'the ministry of the word and prayer'. They have time in a way in which their fellow leaders, unless retired, do not have. As part of their leadership role, they need to use some of this time to think and pray.

Needless to say, such thinking and praying — 'dreaming' — can be hard work. For inspiration does not always involve sudden 'flashes of light'. God expects leaders to use their minds in their search for his will. The operation of God's Spirit does not replace the mind, it simply transforms it. As Richard Lovelace helpfully puts it:

> To relinquish the guiding and superintending function of the intellect in our experience seems pious at first, but in the end this course dehumanises us by turning us into either dependent robots waiting to be programmed by the Spirit's guidance, or whimsical enthusiasts blown about by our hunches and emotions.[8]

The 'vision' needs to be tested

Once a 'vision' of where God would have the church go is received, then that vision needs to be tested. It is tested in the first place by sharing it with one's fellow church leaders. If God's Spirit is guiding one, then normally he guides all.

This process of testing is not always easy. On the one hand, leaders need to encourage faith, but on the other hand they must not quench their people's critical faculties. It can indeed be difficult to discern whether a 'vision' for the church's life is truly of God, or whether it is of man. 'God,' writes Eddie Gibbs, 'does not guarantee to provide a safety net to rescue us from our daredevilry which masquerades for faith.'[9]

Testing is a vital step in the process. No one person can pretend they have a monopoly of the Spirit. Needless to say, testing is made easier where the leadership is truly shared.

Goals are then formulated and shared

Once the overall 'vision' or direction is agreed upon, then together the leaders need to formulate appropriate goals and share them with the church.

In a Baptist context this sharing is in fact part of the testing process. This is the opportunity for the church to 'own' the vision. And goals that are owned are likely to be adhered to.

It is also part of the communication process. People need to know where they are going. To use the imagery of spiritual warfare, the church members need to know the overall strategy that is to be adopted in the battle that is to be fought. In this respect the words of Montgomery are pertinent: 'Every single soldier must know, before he goes into battle, how the little battle he is to fight fits into the larger picture, and how the success of his fighting will influence the battle as a whole.'

The annual church meeting

There is much to be said for the church engaging in an annual goal-setting process. In a Baptist context, the most appropriate setting for this exercise is the 'annual church meeting' (as distinct from the monthly 'church meetings'), when traditionally reports on the past year's work are given. However, in addition to the reports on the past twelve months, pastors could take the opportunity to present goals to be adopted for the coming year. If the goal-setting process outlined above has been followed, then these goals will not be theirs alone, but rather the goals proposed by the leadership team ('deacons' or whoever). If this goal-setting process becomes an annual event, then it means that there will also have to be a backward look. For, as has already been argued, goals to be meaningful need to be evaluated. Yet principally the meeting can be forward looking.

Indeed, not only should the church as a whole set goals for itself, the individual activity groupings within the church could do the same. In fact at the same time as reporting to the annual church meeting on their past achievement, they could also be asked to list their particular goals. Lyle Schaller suggests that each organisation be asked to report responses to questions such as these:

(1) What do you plan to do during the coming year? What are your objectives?

(2) How do these objectives relate to the overall purpose of this church?

(3) What, in specific terms, are the programmes you plan to use to achieve these objectives?

(4) What will be the resources you will need to implement these programmes during the coming year? Which of these resources, including lay volunteers, have been committed to these programmes?[10]

Young people set goals

As an example of what can be done if an individual activity group within the church sets goals, I have taken out from my files a paper setting out the objectives of the youth fellowship at Altrincham Baptist Church in the autumn of 1983. The discerning will discern that not all the goals are as measurable as they might be. The goal-setting procedure could be improved. Nonetheless, it makes interesting reading.

(1) Overall purpose

The purpose of the YF shall be similar to the basic purpose of the church, save that its efforts are directed toward young people: ie, the basic purpose is twofold: (a) *evangelistic*: we seek to win young people for Christ and church; (b) *developmental*: we seek to develop young people in their understanding of the faith, in spiritual growth generally, and in service to the church and the world.

(2) Objectives for autumn 1983

(a) *Evangelistic*

(i) To encourage each Christian young person to introduce at least one friend to the YF this autumn. We will record not only the names of visitors in the visitors' book, but also by whom they were brought along.

(ii)   To run an interesting and varied programme on Sunday evenings, which will appeal to non-Christians. For this purpose we will produce a properly printed programme card.

(iii)   To organise a youth service on Sunday evening 13th November to which YF members could bring their friends *and* their parents.

(iv)   To run a Saturday programme which meets not just the social needs of our own young people, but also the spiritual needs of non-Christians. The programme might be varied, with some Saturdays more intensively evangelistic than others. We propose a 'concert' on Saturday 24th September and Friday 9th December.

(v)   To challenge *individually* each Christian non-member about the claims of baptism and church membership.

(b)   Developmental

(i)   To offer a series of five Bible studies on sharing our faith, to take place on the first five Friday nights of the session.

(ii)   To seek to involve all the Christian members of the YF in Bible study on a Friday night.

(iii)   To take 90% of the YF membership away on a weekend (21st–23rd October).

(iv)   To improve on our present system of pastoral care, mindful of the special needs of those who have just 'moved up' to YF.

(v)   To train up future leadership by giving experience in leading small groups, sharing in occasional leadership meetings, being given limited responsibility for pastoral care (eg, by placing a mature YF member alongside each of the younger members for prayer partnerships).

(vi)   To encourage young people in practical Christian service in such areas as babysitting for church members, taking a service at an old people's home, helping with the party for older friends, serving coffee at the 'Book and Tearcraft Fair' on 15th October.

(vii)   To develop relationships between the young people

and the rest of the church, eg, by inviting older members to take a particular interest in one member or another of the YF — by prayer, looking out for them on a Sunday, inviting them out to tea. NB, this is especially needed by those without Christian homes.

Notes

1. John Stott, *What Is the Spirit Saying?* (Church of England Evangelical Council: Chippenham, Wilts, 1988), p 6.
2. John Stott, *Christian Mission in the Modern World* (Falcon: London, 1975), p 23.
3. *Ibid*, p 29.
4. Colin Marchant, *Signs in the City* (Hodder and Stoughton: London, 1985), p 81.
5. Orlando Costas, *The Church and Its Mission* (Tyndale: Wheaton, IL, 1974), p 90.
6. A A Milne, *Winnie-the-Pooh* (Methuen: 1926).
7. Brian Pearson, *Yes Manager ... Management in the Local Church* (Grove Books: Bramcote, Notts, 1986), pp 7–8.
8. Richard Lovelace, *Dynamics of Spiritual Life* (Paternoster: Exeter, 1979), p 265.
9. Eddie Gibbs, 'Church Growth', *CWR Ministers' Manual* series III, 10, p 4.
10. Lyle Schaller, *op cit*, p 108.

5
Leadership in Action: Achieving the Task

In the last chapter we concentrated on defining the task of the mission of the church. However, it is not enough to define the task and to agree on the goals that serve the overall task. The church also needs to set about actively achieving the task it sets itself. It needs to go for it. However, 'the weakness of the church at present', observes Frank Wright, 'is not so much its lack of vision as its pusillanimity in not acting on insights long ago reached.'[1]

The question therefore arises: how does the leader mobilise the church for action? How does the leader enable the team to fulfil the task? In particular, how does the leader ensure that the church exists for the sake of others rather than itself? How does the leader engage the church in mission, whether mission expresses itself in evangelism or social action?

1. Mobilising the church for evangelism

No true pastor can be unconcerned for the lost. Like the 'Great Shepherd of the sheep', pastors will seek the 'other sheep' who belong to the fold (Jn 10:16). They will want to go in search of the sheep who have gone astray (Mt 18:12–14). Following Paul's injunction to Timothy, they will endeavour to 'do the work of an evangelist' and so 'discharge all the duties' of their ministry (2 Tim 4:5).

However, pastors cannot win the world for Christ on their own — nor should they even attempt it. Their prime task in this respect is to motivate others to share their faith. The 'ordinary' church members are the Lord's front-line troops when it comes to evangelism. Every day they are in touch with 'the world' in a way which many a pastor is simply not. It is they who need to be mobilised.

But how can the troops be mobilised? There seems so much inertia around. 'We have churches of the nicest, kindest people,' wrote P T Forsyth, 'who have nothing apostolic or missionary, who never knew the soul's despair or its breathless gratitude.' Even those churches that call themselves evangelical in doctrine are not necessarily evangelistic in activity. Wilson Carlile, the founder of the Church Army, used to talk of the 'silent saints'. 'I have got the biggest job I have ever tackled in my life. I am trying to open the mouths of the people in the pews.'[2]

In this context, how can pastors bang the evangelism drum with such effect that their people actually go out and make disciples? Clearly there are no easy answers. But the following means have proved helpful.

Arouse prayerful concern in the church

A number of years ago, Hildenborough Hall produced a card emblazoned with the words '*On Target Strategy*'. 'The whole world would be converted in six years if each Christian led one person to Christ each year,' it declared. In graphic form, space was left in the 'bull's eye' of the target for the names of 'six close friends who need Christ' and who 'are my prime responsibility'. Users of the card were encouraged to pray daily for their six unconverted friends, pray together with another Christian who would likewise use the card, and organise their priorities in such a way that they could spend time with their six friends.

Since then, the basic idea of this card has been adapted in

Britain by the Billy Graham Organisation in its popular 'prayer triplets' scheme. However, these prayer triplets lack the world dimension. True, statistics can be misleading, but prayerful concern needs to have the world in view. This was the great beauty of the *On Target Strategy*. If we pray, the world might be saved. It is reminiscent of the early missionary slogan: 'the evangelisation of the world in this generation'.

Concern needs to be aroused for the world in its lostness. The church needs to regain its vision of the world reconciled in Christ (2 Cor 5:19). Within such a context practical steps, such as praying for six unconverted friends, can then be offered.

Every great missionary movement has begun in a context of prayer. People sometimes forget that the modern missionary movement had its beginnings in the 'prayer call' of the Northamptonshire Baptist Association in 1784. This prayer call had five aims:

(1) the spiritual renewal of ministers and churches
(2) the conversion of sinners
(3) the edification of saints
(4) the revival of religion
(5) the glorifying of God's name.

Historians tell us that this prayer call resulted in the birth of the Baptist Missionary Society, and also a growth in village preaching, chapel-building, evangelistic work in Ireland, the founding of colleges for 'ministerial' training and the formation of the Baptist Union of Great Britain and Ireland.

Prayer changes things! *Decision* magazine (the magazine of the Billy Graham Evangelistic Association) once surveyed seventeen outstanding local churches on three continents over a period of several years. One of the characteristics which emerged as common to them all was prayer. 'All the churches studied placed so much emphasis on prayer that it could be said that nothing of importance happened without prayer. Half-nights of prayer, prayer breakfasts, staff prayers, prayer retreats, daily regular and special prayer sessions . . . all part of the pattern, depending on the church.'

Prayer rouses concern. Prayer rouses faith. Prayer becomes the catalyst through which God works. Richard Lovelace, when writing of charismatics, rebukes us all when he says: 'When they commence a venture, it is with hours of prayer, while with ordinary Evangelicals it is with hours of talk and organisation. The result is often that the Charismatics achieve supernatural results, while the rest of us obtain what is organizable.'[3]

Help the newly converted to exploit their networks

In one sense all Christians should be encouraged to work on their networks of relationships. However, the older people grow in the faith, the more likely they are to move into a Christian ghetto. True, this process is not inevitable and could, with imagination and hard work, be reversed. What would happen if pastors suggested that all home groups were suspended for the September–December session and that instead members enroll in evening classes at the local College of Further Education with a view to making friends with some of the happy pagans around? Think of the impact that could be made — especially if each class had several Christians in it!

But to return to the new Christians: they have an immediate network of non-Christian friends to tap into. They may be friends at work, friends down at the pub, or just friends next door. Instead of being encouraged to turn their backs on these friends, they should be encouraged to cultivate them and share their fresh testimony of faith with them. They may need help in this. Part of the strategy of the church might be to encourage new Christians to invite for supper a couple of non-Christian friends together with a couple of new Christian friends.

One would hope that it would not be necessary to motivate new Christians to share their faith. Normally they are bubbling over with the difference that Christ has made to life. However, sometimes they need help to know how to share their faith.

The story is told of how the first Indian bishop, Bishop Azariah, used to get his baptismal candidates to place their hands on their head and say after him: 'I am a baptised Christian. Woe unto me if I preach not the gospel.' The story goes on that once, at a conference, the Bishop asked the participants how many people they had brought to Christ since their baptism. One old woman got up with difficulty and said with apparent sorrow, 'I have only brought five people to Christ since I was baptised.' Only! What a challenge to us.

Offer training in faith-sharing

One way to encourage people to speak for Christ is to offer basic training in faith-sharing. Confidence comes as people learn how to present their faith. It may appear to be a rigid approach to evangelism, but my own experience has shown that people find value in having learnt a gospel outline (the 'skeleton') together with appropriate Scripture verses (the 'muscles'), which they may then be able to 'flesh out' with illustrations drawn from personal experience.

Currently many such training programmes abound on the Christian market. My advice is to take the best of all that is available and then construct a training programme that best fits one's church.

Who should be trained? Ideally everybody. Each person should know how to share his/her faith. However, there is something to be said for being strategic about those to whom one offers such training. In the past I used to seek to enroll automatically the newly-baptised on such training programmes. If I had my time over again in the pastorate, I would now go for the pregnant mums who, in evangelistic potential, form the most strategic group in the church. Without any trying on their part, they find their networks of relationships expanding. Thus in attending ante-natal classes — and later hospital and clinics — they find themselves meeting up with a wide spectrum of people. People, furthermore, who are open to exploring the deeper issues of life.

For mothers at this stage are asking questions as to the meaning and purpose of life. The birth-process is a crisis period in life, when all of a sudden people are jolted out of the ruts of their previous way of thinking and are open to hearing the gospel. Pregnant mums in the church need to be taught how to capitalise on this stage in their life and to use it for winning others to Christ and his church.

Encourage the 'evangelists'

All are called to witness (Acts 1:8), but not all are gifted as evangelists. Some find it easier to share their faith and lead a person to Christ. Peter Wagner, a leading church growth authority, believes that while 10% of Christians have the gift of an 'evangelist', only 0.5% are actually exercising this gift. If this is so, then this is a challenge to any pastor. Wagner likewise believes that the remaining 90% should then be responsible for 'folding' (ie, nurturing) the new convert. This is rather a monochrome approach to the gifts of the Spirit. However, the overall thrust is surely right. Wagner goes on: 'Mobilise the 10% evangelistically gifted and combine them with the new members. The result is maximum evangelistic power.'[4]

How are such gifts discovered? One way is through visitation evangelism. This quickly reveals those who are gifted and those who are not. Once the 'evangelists' are discovered, they should be freed of other responsibilities in the church and encouraged to use their gift in the service of Christ.

Develop an overall evangelistic strategy

A friend of mine once likened the church to a furniture store. He suggested that just as any progressive furniture store has 'special offers' — with each month having a distinctive flavour about it — so too the church must constantly be rearranging its wares. On reflection that analogy seems rather far fetched. And yet is there not some truth in it? Although there is only one basic message to declare, leaders must be prepared to alter their packaging if they are to reach their communities for Christ. Hence the need for a strategy.

The strategy may involve having a 'special' evangelistic service once a month. It may be a 'festival' service linking in to Christmas, Mother's Day, Easter, Whitsun or Harvest. It may be a 'guest' service involving some well-known and/or eminent person sharing their faith. It may involve music (black choirs are always an attraction) or young people (they will bring friends). The most successful 'special' services I have experienced are baptismal services, especially when the pastor has challenged each baptismal candidate to bring along twenty guests ('relatives, friends, and enemies!'). The church is soon packed out with non-Christians.

The strategy may involve mini-missions. Traditionally September has always been regarded as the best time of the year, but there is much to be said for capitalising on the two main Christian festivals, Christmas and Easter. Although both festivals have been commercialised and trivialised, at their roots lie, of course, the Christian gospel. What is more natural than for Christians to spell out their faith at such times as these? Furthermore, many people are open to exploring this gospel that lies at the heart of the world's festivities.

Undoubtedly the strategy will involve outreach to special groups. Thus increasingly it is being recognised that children are becoming a neglected mission-field. Whereas a survey in 1955 revealed that 83% of all adults interviewed admitted that they had prolonged attendance at Sunday school, a similar survey carried out today would reveal a very different state of affairs. The evangelist Gavin Reid has argued that today we are facing a break-up of the moral consensus, which will be of profound significance to future gospel-preaching. In the past people who have responded to evangelistic appeals have often been to Sunday school, where the seed of the gospel had been planted. But if things continue as they are, there will be no harvest to be reaped, for no seed has been sown. Therefore, leaders concerned to reach children with the gospel, will have to develop radical new strategies for winning this age group. Sunday schools in their traditional form are not succeeding. Perhaps week-night specials (not necessarily uniformed organisations) are needed to reach the non-church child.

Another area for strategic sowing of the gospel is to be found among men. At the moment there is an imbalance between the sexes in most churches. In many churches there are two to three women to one man. This presumably means that men are less likely to hear the gospel. Nationally this becomes even more serious when it is realised that in spite of the Equal Opportunities Act, men are still more likely to hold positions of influence in society, which in turn means that Christianity is likely to lose more influence in the nation. The question therefore arises: how can this imbalance be corrected? The traditional men's meetings do not appeal. On the other hand, the 'co-ed' approach to evangelism does not seem to help, for generally men will not open up about their deepest needs before women. Here is an area for strategic thinking — and action. Is the best way to reach men through their 'stomachs', ie, through organising special meals followed by an evangelistic challenge? What is the place for evangelistic study groups specifically targeted at men? Probably there is a place for both — and for more!

So whether the special group be children, men, young people, young marrieds, ladies, or older people, strategic thinking and action is called for. The motto of the church should continue to be 'by all means save some'!

2. Mobilising the church for social action

The task is mission. And mission, I have argued, must include commitment to social action. Just as mission is lopsided if it excludes evangelism, so it is equally lopsided if its focus is only evangelism. Evangelicals still need to hear this loud and clear.

Compassion demands that we are concerned for the social needs of the world around us. Just as Jesus cared for the poor, the sick, the oppressed, and those on the margins of society, so too pastors will be concerned for all those who are in one way or another deprived. The kingdom's boundaries go far beyond the church.

However, and this is crucial, pastors cannot and should not seek to meet the needs of the community on their own. Indeed, in this respect their prime task is not to act as unpaid social workers, but rather to mobilise the church to care. As with evangelism, so too with social action, the task belongs to the church.

But how do leaders mobilise their churches to care? Again as with evangelism, this is no easy challenge. There is an innate selfishness in so many of us. However, the following means may prove helpful.

Arouse prayerful concern in the church

As with evangelism, so too with social concern — prayer is the key. Sunday's concerns should never be limited to matters of personal piety. The world in all its need must be in view.

Prayerful concern will at times be reflected in the pastor's preaching. For preaching must address all the issues of life — of life, among other things, as perceived in the United Nations, the EEC Commission, and the Houses of Parliament. This is not to equate preaching with political commentary. But preaching that totally avoids political issues in fact avoids some of the great moral issues of the day. Charles Elliott has somewhere written some challenging words about this: 'A Spirit-filled church that rejoices in tongues and warm fellowship of the Spirit, but neglects the hard task of prophesying against the powers of darkness as they manifest themselves in our society opens itself to the question of whether it is being faithful to the Spirit in which it exists.' We rightly condemn our pietistic brothers and sisters of a past generation who failed to speak out against

Hitler and his treatment of the Jews, but may some of today's evangelical churches not be in danger of incurring the condemnation of future generations by their apparent failure to address the moral issues of today?

Along with the preaching also goes the praying. World, national and community concerns will not feature in every sermon, but they will surely feature in the regular prayers of the church. If prayers are to be truly Christian, then they will inevitably go beyond the needs of the church and extend to the wider world. Here leadership needs to be exercised. For leadership needs to ensure that prayers are outward looking, covering the full spectrum of concerns. This does not mean that the leading of the prayers of intercession should always be in the hands of pastors. Hopefully they will involve others. However, their task is to ensure that the prayers are indeed broadbased in their concern. In this way concern will be aroused not just for the corporate prayers of the church on a Sunday, but almost certainly for the individual prayers of the congregation through the week. It is surprising how instructive and influential the corporate praying of the church can be in the lives of individuals.

Support 'professionals' in community service

All churches have a sprinkling, if not more than a sprinkling, of people professionally involved in community service. Here I have in mind not just social workers, but teachers, policemen, prison officers, health visitors, doctors, nurses, and many other occupations. Many of these people are at the 'sharp end' of life. It is not easy, for instance, being a teacher or a social worker these days. Suspicion, misunderstanding and confrontation are part of the staple diet of many involved in the community. It is therefore important for a pastor to give special support to such members, particularly when the going gets rough. However, the role of giving support should not be limited to the pastor. What a difference it makes when those involved in particularly difficult situations feel the love and encouragement of the church.

They need to have opportunity to express their concerns publicly — and then to be prayed for publicly too. The leader needs to ensure that the church as a church is involved in supporting those of the membership involved professionally in community service.

Encourage 'volunteers' in community service

Here I have in mind not just WRVS and their excellent meals-on-wheels service, but also the magistracy, the local council, PTAs and school-governing boards. All these — and more — are areas in which Christians can and should be involved.

However, such involvement should not just be left to individual initiative. Nor should it be simply encouraged by general words from the pulpit. Rather the wise leader, together with others, will seek to spot potential within the church, and then directly encourage individuals to get involved in whatever aspect of social activity is in mind. Thus every church should aim to have at least one of its members on the 'bench'. There is no reason why leaders could not spot someone gifted in that direction and then get the church as a church to nominate their candidate to those responsible for selecting magistrates. It may well be that in encouraging people to get involved in the community, the church will be depriving itself of people to service some of its internal activities. But provided there is a balance, what does it matter if a potential leader of the women's work finds herself serving instead outside the church? It is all part of mission.

Encourage involvement in the political process.

In one sense those involved in politics may be deemed as serving the community. However, this is such a needy area of Christian service that it demands treatment on its own. Christians are desperately needed in the political process — whether at local or national level.

No church can dare identify itself with one particular party, for no one political party can ever be fully representative of the gospel. It is hoped that the local church will be represented in all the local political parties.

But how can Christians be best encouraged to get involved in the political process? For there is no doubt that were Christians to get involved, a political revolution would take place. Just imagine if the churches stopped all their mid-week meetings and encouraged their members to get involved in local political parties. The latter, which for the most part are poorly attended, would be overwhelmed by Christians!

An indefinite moratorium of church activity would not be feasible — nor would it be right. But what about an occasional 'fasting' from church activities? For Christians of a certain persuasion, a form of Lenten discipline is to engage in Bible study. I am tempted to suggest that a good Lenten discipline for evangelicals would be to abstain from Bible study and get involved in the local political parties. One or two might get permanently involved!

Encourage the church as a church to serve the community

Not only does the church need to serve the community through the involvement of its individual members, it also needs to be seen as a church that cares. Projects need to be found which, on the one hand offer an avenue of Christian service for its members, and on the other hand offer an opportunity for the church to demonstrate in a practical and concrete way the love of God in Christ.

All manner of projects are possible. Some projects may be long-term (eg, a luncheon club for the elderly; a mothers'-and-toddlers' club); others may be occasional or one-offs (eg, raising money for a local old folks' home; caring one December Saturday for mentally handicapped children so that parents can do their Christmas shopping). The important thing is that 'by all means' the church is seen to care — and indeed, above all, does care!

Conclusion

Evangelism and social action both form an essential part of the church's mission, and therefore both must engage the attention of pastors as they seek to lead out their churches in mission.

Let me conclude this section with a quotation from the Grand Rapids report *Evangelism and Social Responsibility* (p 24).

To proclaim Jesus as Lord and Saviour [evangelism] has social implications, since it summons people to repent of social as well as personal sins, and to live a new life of righteousness and peace in the new society which challenges the old.

To give food to the hungry [social responsibility] has evangelistic implications, since good works of love, if done in the name of Christ, are a demonstration and commendation of the Gospel.

It has been said, therefore, that evangelism, even when it does not have a primarily social intention, nevertheless has a social dimension, while social responsibility, even when it does not have a primarily evangelistic intention, nevertheless has an evangelistic dimension.

Notes

1. Frank Wright, *The Pastoral Nature of the Ministry* (SCM: London, 1980) p 23.
2. John Stott, *Our Guilty Silence* (Hodder and Stoughton: London, 1967) p 13.
3. Richard Lovelace, *Dynamics of Spiritual Life* (Paternoster: Exeter, 1979) p 237.
4. Peter Wagner, *Your Church Can Grow* (Regal Books: Glendale, CA, 1976) p 77.

6

Leadership in Action: The Team

We return again to our definition of a leader: 'A good leader works as a senior partner with other members to achieve the task, build the team and meet individual needs.' In the last two chapters we have focused on the task. We now turn to focus on the team.

1.   The church is the team

In the first instance, the church is the team. It is with this team that the pastor — the church's leader — is called to work.

Welding the team together

To call the church a team may at first sight seem to be stretching a point. David Cormack, for example, writes: 'Two's a company, three's a team, and more than fifteen's a crowd.'[1] According to this definition, most churches are definitely not teams. I disagree. I see one of the key roles of a pastor as welding together what may appear initially to be a motley crew, each doing his or her own thing, into a team, working together to achieve a common task.

I do not pretend that such a welding together is at all easy. Furthermore, the larger a church, the more difficult the welding together becomes. Cormack's list of 'disadvantages in larger teams' is indeed not a little daunting:

1. Difficulty in selecting people who all fit.
2. The likelihood of frequent membership change.
3. Finding roles and tasks for each member which match their skills.
4. Communication between so many allows for misinterpretation.
5. Arranging meeting times acceptable to all.
6. Developing relationships (in a team of 15 there are 210 sets of one-to-one relationships!).
7. Developing members' skills.
8. Allowing sufficient time for members to contribute.
9. The dangers of sub-group formation and conflict.

Yet these disadvantages are not insuperable. Let's examine them one by one.

(i) 'Difficulty in selecting people who all fit.' In one sense this is totally inapplicable. Pastors cannot hand-pick their members. Rather, if anything the reverse is true. In the first place it is the church which selects the pastor — although the pastor always has the freedom to accept or not accept the 'call'. Yet for all that, there is an element of membership selection. In Baptist churches, for instance, the church meeting is responsible for accepting new members into the church. The basis for acceptance is their commitment to the Lord Jesus and their desire to commit themselves to this particular local church. Indeed, the very application for church membership involves a certain measure of self-selection. Nonetheless, such selection procedures do not guarantee homogeneity — nor would we want them to. It is hoped that they would result in a body of people all 'facing the same direction'.

(ii) 'The likelihood of frequent membership change.' In my last year as pastor of a local church, the church's membership-roll changed by a third. Such mobility may be

exceptional, yet it illustrates the problem. How do you construct a sense of identity in a church whose membership is so mobile? One way of overcoming the problem is by running classes for new members, in which the ethos of the church and its overall direction is outlined. In this way new members, as they commit themselves to the church, will be committing themselves in a conscious fashion to a particular understanding of the church's task.

(iii) 'Finding roles and tasks for each member which match their skills.'   Yes, it is a challenge in a large church to ensure that every member is engaged in appropriate ministry. In a large church it is more easily possible for members to behave like passengers rather than active members of the crew. But where a church is broken down into small groups, every-member ministry is more than feasible, not least within the context of that small group. Large churches need not inhibit every-member ministry. Indeed, one may argue that the larger a church is, the more it is able to accomplish for Christ.

(iv) 'Communication between so many allows for mis-interpretation.'   Yes, indeed it does. Communication in a body of any size is a problem. What is more, this problem is not overcome simply by the issuing of weekly newsletters and generally shifting pieces of paper around, for there is no guarantee that such written information will ever be read. Face-to-face communication is the best medium of communication. This can be done from the pulpit, or it may be done through small groups. At the end of the day, however, it needs to be recognised that the key to good communication within a church context is not just to say it once, but to say it several times. Somehow messages are never heard unless they are repeated!

(v) 'Arranging meeting times acceptable to all.'   Within a church context this does not pose a problem. The hours of

Sunday worship, as also the time of the mid-week meeting or house group, are 'givens' which most people can simply write into their diaries.

(vi) 'Developing relationships.' There is a limit to the number of relationships that can be developed at any depth. Thus, according to Peter Cotterell, eighty is 'the maximum number of people who can adequately get to know one another by name, to relate in a measure to one another. Beyond this size some members will be inevitably overlooked.'[2]

However, this does not mean that a church with more than eighty members need cease to be a cohesive community — not if commitment to the 'team' (ie, the body, the church) and to the task is constantly emphasised, both from the pulpit as within the house groups and new members' classes. Furthermore, although relationships will be developed primarily within the small groups, there is a sense in which relationships with the leaders are strengthened every Sunday. For, however large the crowd attending Sunday worship, there is a sense in which the pastor and any others involved in up-front leadership enter into a one-to-one relationship with each member of the congregation through the act of leading the worship and preaching the word. The leaders may not always be aware that they are entering into such a relationship, but their people most certainly are.

(vii) 'Developing members' skills.' This is perhaps the hardest of the nine 'disadvantages' listed by David Cormack. Furthermore, not only is it the hardest, but experience shows that often it is the most neglected. Traditionally pastors have been very poor in providing opportunities for members to develop their gifts and skills. Yet even where such opportunities are offered — either by providing programmes within the local church itself or drawing attention to programmes organised from without, it is not always easy getting members to attend and take advantage of what is on offer.

(viii) 'Allowing sufficient time for members to contribute.'
Yes, the dynamics between a church meeting with 15 members present and a church meeting with 150 members present are very different. Clearly, in such a context not everybody can be heard by all. Hence the desirability of leaders of larger church meetings ensuring that from time to time the gathering is broken up into small buzz groups where the voice of even the shyest can be heard and, if deemed right, later communicated to the larger company.

(ix) 'The dangers of sub-group formation and conflict.' The inference here is that the sub-groups produce conflict. But this is not necessarily so. Sub-groups become dangerous when they are not organised or when cliques are allowed to form, for cliques can indeed become partisan. Leaders of larger churches should ensure that their church is broken down into organised small groups which are then 'controlled' from the centre, in the sense that such groups are given a unifying purpose as they seek to achieve a common task.

To return to our thesis. The church is the team. The role of the pastor-leader is to ensure that it becomes and remains a team. There is no let-up in this task. Teamsmanship must be constantly worked at. Paul's words in Ephesians 4:3 regarding unity are very relevant: 'Make every effort to keep the unity of the Spirit through the bond of peace.' It is an ongoing effort. The church is already a team, yet it must remain a team. It must constantly become what it already is. Here the role of the leader is crucial. Negatively, the leader is called to troubleshoot. Thus when relationship difficulties arise — and such difficulties are inevitable, for the church is made up of fallible men and women — then the leader must be unafraid to deal with such difficulties, to confront those who need to be confronted, so that healing and harmony may prevail again. More positively, the leader must constantly seek to weld the team together by giving it a sense of common purpose and direction. Indeed, the task itself is a unifying force.

Introducing change to the team

But is the task always a unifying force? Strangely, in spite of what I have just said, the task can sometimes prove to be a disuniting force. It can prove disuniting when, with a view to the church becoming more effective in its mission, ie, in achieving its task, the leader proposes changes to the way in which the team operates. Such changes are not always welcome.

This may sound strange, for from a theoretical point of view churches should take to change like a duck to water. After all, in a very real sense churches are in the business of change. We call men and women to repent, and to repent is to change. Yet sadly, although the gospel means change, Christians all too often seem to resist change. Indeed, the more conservative Christians are in their theology, the more conservative many of them are towards new ideas. Logically, this is contradictory. If anything, with such a revolutionary gospel, 'Bible-believing' Christians should be among the most radical. In practice, alas, they are often not.

What has happened, of course, is that the church has become an organisation, and organisations tend towards stability. The movement has become a monument. In the words of Peter Drucker: 'Left to themselves, institutions develop resistance to change. In a service institution particularly, yesterday's success becomes today's policy, virtues, conviction, if not holy writ, unless the institution imposes on itself the discipline of thinking through its mission.'[3] It is so easy for a church to settle down into a rut and be complacent with the status quo and fail to see the need for radical change. Hence the need for leadership! Leadership which is conscious of the need to achieve the task. As it is:

> Since most Christian organisations continue to exist because of the favourable perception of their supporters rather than their necessary performance in the marketplace of life, it is all too easy for them to succumb to the idea that their lack of progress is God's will for them. One of the roles of the change agent [ie, the

leader] is to help people see that God desires them to be growing, not only in their individual lives, but in the life of their organisation.[4]

But how does one handle change in a church? It is not enough for leaders to be aware of the need for change. They must be able to handle the process of change. Alas, many a good idea has foundered and many a church has been split because leaders have not understood the dynamics involved in the process of change. In the down-to-earth language of Eddie Gibbs, it is all too easy to break eggs without succeeding in making omelettes. As Machiavelli, *The Prince*, recognised long ago:

> There is nothing more difficult to carry out, nor more doubtful of success, nor more dangerous to handle, than to initiate a new order of things. For the reformer has enemies in all who profit by the old order, and only luke-warm defenders in all those who profit by the new order. This luke-warmness arises partly from fear of their adversaries, who have law in their favour, and partly from the incredulity of mankind, who do not truly believe in anything new until they have actual experience of it.[5]

Change involves a process

Change involves far more than the wave of a magic wand; it involves a whole series of steps. EM Rogers and FF Shoemaker in *The Communication of Innovations* (Collier Macmillan: New York, 1971), a classic book on the introduction of change, present a four-stage model for the process of change: Knowledge, Persuasion, Decision and Confirmation. I shall follow this scheme as I seek to develop the role of the leader in bringing about change.

(i) Knowledge. A church needs to understand why the proposed change is necessary and what will be involved.

Let's take this in two stages. First, the church needs to understand why the change is necessary. This is the key to the process of change, for change will only be accepted if it is seen to be truly necessary. Indeed, it may be argued that change takes place in direct proportion to the sense of need. Thus Dayton and Engstrom write:

> People only like to change when they are discontented. It may be a broad and holy discontent, leading to a wish to see the world a more God-honouring place — or it may be a desire to remove a minor discomfort or annoyance. As Sol Alinskey, the famous union organizer, used to say, 'Rub the bruises sore.' He was focusing on the fact that you have to begin with the discontent and build on that.[6]

For leaders to begin to bring about change, they must make their people aware of the difficulties or drawbacks of their present position. It is only, for instance, when they perceive some of the disadvantages of meeting for Sunday morning worship at 11 am, that the church can begin to think that an earlier time might be more advantageous.

But a sense of need is not enough. Direction is also necessary. The church must clearly understand the change that is being proposed. For instance, the leader may propose that in view of the large number of young families attending church, it would be helpful to begin Morning Worship at 10 am. Change always involves an element of uncertainty. It is essential therefore to spell out the steps which must be taken and the end which will be achieved.

(ii) Persuasion. It is not enough for people to understand the change that is being proposed. They need to be persuaded that this is a change they must take on board. In so far as most people do not welcome change of any kind, it should not be surprising if the initial responses are negative — this is the way things always are.

Persuasion is often best carried out on a one-to-one basis or in small informal groups. The church meeting is not the best place for the initial persuasion process, for the simple reason that by and large public responses are likely to be permanent. It is much more difficult to get folk to retract publicly stated positions. The wise leader will therefore need to seek out and talk privately to the 'opinion leaders' in the church, particularly when the pastor is young or newly arrived in the church. Change takes place best in an atmosphere of trust. If the trusted senior deacon is in favour of a proposed change, then the church as a whole is likely to follow. To attempt to bring about change without gaining the support of the 'opinion leaders' in the church is to invite disaster.

Another useful vehicle for the persuasion process is house groups. Here, within the informal context of a home setting, it is possible to debate freely the proposed changes without feeling the constraint of standing by any expressed opinion. At this stage there is a fluidity in the discussion. However, if house groups are to talk about proposed changes in the church, then it is vital for the leaders to have gained the prior support of the house-group leaders. Otherwise, if they are not convinced, more harm than good can come out of discussion within the house groups.

As for the method one adopts to persuade others, it is important to realise that few people are truly objective. Change is normally evaluated in personal terms ('This is how it will affect me') before it is assessed in terms of the whole church. This means that there is much to be said in presenting the benefits of change in personal terms: 'This is how it will affect *you*.' The wise leader will therefore combine both a subjective and an objective approach.

(iii) *Decision.* At some stage the church needs to adopt or reject the proposed change. For Baptists this decision takes place at the church meeting. If the change is of any significance, however, then it is important that a decision is not made at the church meeting at which it is proposed. Time needs to be given before the decision is made. This applies even if the matter has already been talked through informally in some of the house groups. Let the church know that at

the next church meeting a decision will be taken. In this way the church will feel free to talk about the proposed change without a sense of threat. In the words of Larry Richards: 'The success of change in a church depends on the personal spiritual growth of the church members and on their sense of freedom to take part openly and honestly in the change process.'[7]

(iv) Confirmation. Finally, after the change has taken place, the church needs to be able to affirm the decision that was made. To this end the wise leader will let the members know that after so many months the church will have an opportunity to reflect upon, and if necessary revise, changes that have been made. This course of action makes change an easier prospect for those who are conservative. They perceive proposed changes as experiments, rather than as something fixed for all time. The fact that the proposed change need not be permanent, somehow makes it easier for change to be adopted. But once the changes have been adopted and proved successful, then it is good to allow the church to affirm the wisdom of its earlier decision!

Change involves time

'Churches,' it has been said, 'are a lot like horses. They don't like to be startled or surprised. It causes deviant behaviour.' In other words, changes cannot suddenly be sprung on people. Or if they are, then they will not work and will not be accepted. The wise leader needs to recognise that change in church life needs time and patience. In the words of Michael Saward: 'Generals can act like God; pastors have to act like God incarnate. Creation takes more than six days for them.'[8] Change often needs months of careful preparation and persuasion. Good ideas can often be wrecked and churches split if a pastor forces a church to take a decision before it is truly ready to take that decision.

Here again the work of EM Rogers and FF Shoemaker is most helpful. For in their work on the acceptance of change they have shown that there are various rates of adoption and categories of adopters. These have been classified in the following terms:

1. *Innovators*. These comprise 2.5% of the group receiving the change. They are enthusiastic about and promote its introduction to the group.
2. *Early Adopters*. These form a further 13.5% of the group. They are quick to accept the change, are happy with it and promote its introduction.
3. *Early Majority*. These form a further 24% of the group. A total of half now accept the change. Many have had reservations but have been persuaded and now persuade others.
4. *Late Majority*. A further 34%. Most were initially resistant to the change, but have been gradually won over.
5. *Laggards*. The final 16% who now accept the change grudgingly. The dissidents remain in this group even after the change has become tradition!

This is a most helpful analytical tool. Some of the percentages may be questioned — personally I find the figure for 'Laggards' unduly high. Lyle Schaller, for instance, is on record as saying that only 'about 3% of church members enjoy intimidating the pastor'![9] However, I find the general drift of the argument convincing. In particular, it shows the dangers of a leader forcing a church to come to a decision too rapidly. Many churches have, for instance, been split unnecessarily over the question of charismatic renewal. It is all too easy for impatient pastors to force a vote when they have only 50% of the church behind them. With a little more time and patience, they could have got the Late Majority — ie, a further 34% — behind them too.

Change is never immediately welcome

As the previous sections indicate, change is never immediately welcome. For the most part people initially resist change. They are much happier with the status quo. There is an amusing story which tells of a new pastor's conversation with one of his senior deacons. 'You must have seen a number of changes in this church,' began the young pastor. 'Yes,' replied the deacon, 'and I've opposed every one of them.'

Why don't people welcome change? What causes them to resist the new? The Bible Society, in its *Advanced Course for Church Growth*, Unit 2/5, listed eight obstacles to change.

1. *Lack of biblical understanding*. Many people resist change because they fail to understand the issues. Careful and systematic exposition of the biblical basis for change will be necessary.
2. *Disobedience*. Right knowledge does not guarantee right action. Today many churches miss the purpose and blessing of God because they are unwilling to obey him, preferring their own way.
3. *Tradition*. Many follow the traditions of men rather than the teachings of God. This was a problem in ancient Israel and even our Lord had to warn against it. It remains a serious problem today, whether the traditions date from the Middle Ages or the turn of the century.
4. *Fear of the new*. Love of the old and familiar often produces fear of anything new. People feel threatened by change and irrationally oppose it.
5. *Errors of timing*. Many leaders misjudge the timing and pace of change and encounter obstacles of their own creation.
6. *Lack of confidence in the leadership*. Major change can only be introduced by leaders who have taken time to establish respect and trust.
7. *Polarisation*. Dissent leads to division and disunity which may produce factions, each defending a particular issue and opposing the change for different reasons.
8. *Inadequate planning*. Attempts to reach long-term goals without the achievement of a series of short-term goals lead to frustration and failure.

How do we evaluate these 'obstacles'? No doubt in some

churches obstacles 1 ('the lack of biblical understanding') and 2 ('disobedience') are factors, but these obstacles are far less frequently found than some leaders would have us believe. Probably in most churches obstacles 3 ('tradition') and 4 ('fear of the new') are more relevant. However, these obstacles are not insuperable. Leaders should seek to remind their people of Abraham and of God's call to them to be the pilgrim people of God. In the words of Philip King: 'The task of the Christian leader is to wean people from dependence on an unchanging church life to dependence on an unchanging God.'[10]

Of the remaining obstacles, 5 ('errors of timing') and 6 ('lack of confidence in leadership') are perhaps the most important. Time and time again leaders blame their people for resistance to change, whereas in fact the blame may lie on them and their failure to understand the process of change. Change takes time — this cannot be stressed too much. Furthermore, change is bound up with relationships. For ultimately change is not about programmes but about people. People are prepared to change if they feel that they can trust their leader(s).

There is, however, one final obstacle missing from the Bible Society's list. I agree with Marshall Shelley that people often resist changes because 'they demonstrate that someone else has more power, and *they* are creating changes *we* have to live by'.[11] In other words, change is all right if we are actually initiating it — but it is not at all right if someone else is seen to be imposing it! If this is so, all the more reason for the leader to ensure that when major changes are brought about, they are seen and felt to be the work of the church meeting.

2. The team meeting together (the church meeting)

Reference has already been made on a number of occasions to the church meeting. It is now time to deal with this institution of congregational church government at greater depth. I am particularly interested in examining the church meeting from the perspective of the leader who is seeking to achieve the task, build the team, and meet the needs of individuals.

In the last decade or two, the Baptist church meeting has had a bad press. Much scorn has been heaped on it, not least by former Baptists who have joined Restoration groups. Perhaps some of the scorn has been deserved. There is no doubt that in some places the church meeting has degenerated into a mere business meeting at which the will of the people (democracy) rather than the will of God (theocracy) has constantly triumphed. However, it needs to be said that at times some of the criticism has been unjust. 'Aunt Sallies' have been created by caricaturing church meetings, with the result that such Aunt Sallies have easily been knocked down. The real thing, however, is much more difficult to knock down.

God at work

At its best, the church meeting 'is the occasion when as individuals and as a community the members submit themselves to the guidance of the Holy Spirit and stand under the judgment of God that they may know what is the mind of Christ' (taken from the 1948 Baptist Union Statement). It is, in the terms of this book, the team meeting together, seeking guidance for the task.

This understanding of the church meeting accords with three basic scriptural principles.

(i) The lordship of Christ. First and foremost the church is not, as some of my own fellow Baptists have argued, 'the fellowship of believers'. It is rather, in the words of JH Oldham, 'Jesus Christ at work in the world through the fellowship of redeemed sinners'. Or to put the thought more simply in biblical terms, the church is the body of Christ (1 Cor 12:27; Eph 4:12), the bride of Christ (Rev 19:7), and the temple of the Spirit (1 Cor 6:19). The church — whether local or universal — is only the church in so far as it relates to

Christ as its Redeemer and its Head. Therefore in its life together the church is not called to be democratic or despotic, but Christocentric. Jesus must be Lord!

(ii) The priesthood of all believers. This principle, enunciated in 1 Peter 2:4–5, 9, declares that the age-old distinction between priest and people has been superseded. We are all priests! In Godward terms this means that there is no need for any human mediator between God and man: Jesus is the one mediator (1 Tim 2:5). In spiritual terms we are all equal before God. No one cadre has a greater claim on the Holy Spirit than another. In manward terms we are called to represent Christ to one another and the world. For this is the priestly task: to build bridges between God and his world. In the light of these two aspects of priesthood, there is good ground for believing that every church member can be open to God and his word. No one spiritual elite can claim to have a special hot-line to God!

(iii) The ministry of all believers. No doubt a number of passages could be cited supporting this doctrine, but the chapter which particularly comes to mind is 1 Corinthians 12, where Paul develops the picture of the church as a body. Paul is here saying that God has so designed the body that the involvement of every person with his or her special gift is necessary for the proper function of the community. Every member has a unique role to play. Indeed, the body is weaker where members withdraw and leave others to do the running! Yes, there are particular leadership roles given by God to certain individuals, but these individuals in no way have a monopoly of the Holy Spirit. For best results all God's people are needed to pull together.

These principles are reinforced by Luke's description of the early church in action. When decisions of fundamental importance had to be made, the whole church was involved in seeking the mind of Christ. Three examples come to mind.

(a)   When the first 'deacons' were appointed, it was left to the church — and not to the Apostles — to choose seven men 'known to be full of the Spirit and of wisdom. ... They presented these men to the apostles, who prayed and laid their hands on them' (Acts 6:3, 6). Surely it is not anachronistic to say that the church meeting was involved?

(b)   Again, at the Jerusalem Council called to discuss the whole question of admission of Gentile members, although the Apostles and the elders took the initiative in thrashing the matter through, the church as a whole was involved in making the decision to welcome Gentile believers into their midst. Luke records that 'the apostles and the elders, with the whole church, decided' (Acts 15:22). Indeed, later in that chapter he quoted the letter from the Jerusalem Council which described that decision in terms of it seeming 'good to the Holy Spirit and to us' (Acts 15:28). God guided his people through prayerful discussion together.

(c)   My third example of the church acting together is found in Acts 11, in the context of finance. Having heard Agabus' word from the Lord, 'the disciples, each according to his ability, decided to provide help for the brothers living in Judea. This they did, sending their gift to the elders by Barnabas and Saul' (Acts 11:29-39). It is, of course, dangerous to read into the silences of Scripture: nonetheless, it does seem significant that the disciples — and not the elders alone — were involved in the decision-making process. In other words, whether in the election of church officers, the admission of members, or the administration of finance, the church as a church was involved.

The experience of the early church, however, is not sufficient. Our final authority must surely be the Lord Jesus himself. Here Matthew 18:15-20 is the foundational text. The ultimate recourse in church discipline is not the elders but the church. When an erring brother refuses to listen to you, and you have gone on to try and speak to him in the presence of one or two others, then, says Jesus, you are to 'tell it to the church' which has authority to bind and loose, because Jesus is in the midst!

Interestingly, we have an example of this practice being carried out in Paul's first letter to the Corinthians. 'When you are assembled [ie, in what we would call the church meeting] ... hand this man over to Satan, so that the sinful nature may be destroyed and his spirit saved on the day of the Lord Jesus' (1 Cor 5:4–5). Whatever else this difficult passage may mean, one thing is for sure: if 'the behaviour of an individual Christian has affected the life of a local church (either through the prominence of that individual or widespread knowledge of such behaviour in the congregation as a whole), there discipline needs to be exercised and explained when the church as a whole is gathered together'.[12] Furthermore, it is discipline exercised not by the elders, but by the church. The final authority lies within the church meeting.

The leader's authority

On this model of church life, the church meeting becomes the ultimate decision-making body. What an exciting model it is! Every member has a part to play. Every member counts. What a demanding model it is, too! It expects much from the membership. For in this view of church life, church membership has little to do with a name being on a roll. Rather, it has everything to do with commitment — to Christ and to one another. Furthermore, if this model of the church is dependent on a high view of church membership, it is also dependent on a high view of the church meeting itself. Thus at such church meetings church business cannot be limited to rubber-stamping decisions relating to finance and fabric. Instead it involves the seeking of the mind of Christ in relation to all matters of faith and practice. There is nothing which is outside the orbit of the church meeting.

But where do leaders fit into all this? There is clearly an element of tension. On the one hand, leaders are to lead the flock of God and as such are accountable to the Lord himself (Heb 13:17). As Paul emphasised to the Galatians, leaders are in the first place servants of God, and not servants of men (Gal 1:10). Similarly, in Ephesians 4:11 it is Christ who 'gives' pastor-teachers to his church, which in turn means that it is from Christ that pastor-teachers derive their authority, and it is to Christ that they owe their allegiance. Yet, on the other hand, leaders are accountable to the church, which has recognised their calling and set them apart for service (Acts 13:1–3; 14:27). As we have already seen, ultimate authority rests in the meeting together of the church's members (Mt 18:15–20). How, then, do we resolve this tension? The simple answer is that we cannot. The presence of tension is no argument for doing away with it — otherwise, where would some of our great doctrines of the faith be? Accountability does not rob the pastoral office of authority. Rightly understood, the church in appointing its leaders has delegated to them authority, authority which the leaders are free to exercise until the church withdraws its recognition of them.

The leader's role

Within the context of the church meeting, pastors have a key role to play. Three aspects of their role may be seen in:

(i) *Setting the agenda.*   Pastors have a key role in drawing up the agenda of a church meeting. If the church meeting is the place for discerning the mind of Christ, then this means that items like the colour of the new ladies' toilet do not belong there. The church meeting is the place for items of substance like evangelism and social action. Small matters can be delegated to the deacons to deal with.

(ii) *Creating the atmosphere.*   Pastors have a key role to play in chairing the church meeting. They are not simply there to ensure that fair play takes place, but also to give a positive lead. I'm not convinced that Steve Gaukroger is right in suggesting that pastors need to be 'a sort of "Wogan at worship"', but they are called to set the right tone. Steve

Gaukroger makes three positive suggestions as far as the pastor's role is concerned.

* Avoid the great worship versus business divide

'Worship is not to be treated as the preliminaries, which have to be gone through before one can get down to the business in hand. Worship should permeate the whole of the agenda.' Exactly! There is much to be said for having fifteen minutes of prayer halfway through the agenda. By that stage people have been given fuel for prayer. Furthermore, it does away with that unfortunate syndrome whereby some people turn up late because they don't regard the opening worship as belonging to the guts of the meeting.

* Keep it fresh

'Let different people take part. Use the overhead projector for reports. . . . Change seating arrangements. Break up into discussion groups.' Nothing is worse than having just two or three people at the front dominating the proceedings. Pastors have their work cut out in ensuring there is variety.

* Be positive

'Even when discussing difficult issues keep a positive approach. . . . Never lose your temper. . . . Set (and keep!) the tone for the whole meeting.' There are indeed times when the patience of pastors is sorely tested. They are tempted to let fly or be cutting. But such behaviour never wins the day.[13]

(iii) Exercising helmsmanship. I have already referred to this role of the pastor when examining 1 Corinthians 12:28 and the so-called gift of 'administration'. One of the tasks of pastors is to have their hand on the tiller, allowing the church to respond to the guidance of the Holy Spirit. As words of wisdom and/or 'prophecy' are shared within the context of the church meeting, it is the task of the leader to ensure that words are tested and weighed. Great sensitivity is required in this task. It involves listening — and not all leaders find it easy to listen when they are concerned to push through some scheme of their own. The church meeting, however,

demands that all who are present are open to God — the pastor included. (Incidentally, precisely because openness and listening are involved, this means that the custom some churches have of postal voting is a theological nonsense.)

Let me conclude this section on the church meeting with two quotations. First, from a Baptist pastor: 'The Church Meeting is not a papal audience, nor is it a "Parliamentary" party battle ground. It is the family of God rejoicing in its response to visionary and loving leadership, in worship, in prayer, and in mutual submission to each other under God.'[14]

Or, in the words of the great Congregational preacher of times past, RW Dale: 'To be at a church meeting is for me one of the chief means of grace.' Of course, there are times when the church meeting is less than it should be, but given the right leadership there can be no finer instrument for helping the church to discover the mind of Christ.

Notes

1. David Cormack, *Team Spirit* (MARC: Bromley, 1987), p 20.
2. Peter Cotterell, *The Eleventh Commandment* (InterVarsity Press: Leicester, 1981), p 50.
3. Peter Drucker, *Management* (Harper and Row: New York, 1974), p 523.
4. David Cormack, *Managing Change* (MARC: Bromley), p 71.
5. Eddie Gibbs, *I Believe in Church Growth* (Hodder and Stoughton: London, 1981), p 427.
6. Edward Dayton and Ted Engstrom, *Strategy for Leadership* (MARC: Bromley, 1985), p 114.
7. Larry Richards, quoted in Lloyd Perry, *Getting the Church on Target* (Moody: Chicago, Il, 1977), p 119.
8. Michael Saward, *All Change* (Hodder and Stoughton: London, 1983), p 40.
9. Lyle Schaller, article in *Grid* (autumn 1987).
10. Philip King, *Leadership Explosion* (Hodder and Stoughton: London, 1987), p 151.
11. Marshall Shelley, *Leadership* vii.4.1.

12. David Prior, *The Message of 1 Corinthians* (InterVarsity Press: Leicester, 1985), p 74.
13. Steve Gaukroger, 'Renewing the Church Meeting', *Mainstream* no 26 (September 1987), pp 5–7.
14. Frank Cooke, article in *The Fraternal* (July 1985), p 9.

7
Leadership in Action: Teams Within the Team

From the 'team' (the church) we now turn to the teams within the 'team' with which pastors have to work. Here we have in mind the various leadership teams found in churches. My concern in this chapter is to explore the ways in which pastors can develop these teams, with a view to achieving the overall task or mission of the church.

1. The leadership team (the deacons)

The majority of churches have one basic leadership team. The name that is given to this team varies: some churches talk of the oversight, others of the elders, yet others of the deacons. For sake of ease I will use the term that is most widely used in Baptist churches: the deacons. For sake of clarity I would emphasise that when I speak of 'deacons' I do not have in mind a management committee which simply cares for the day-to-day business of the church on behalf of the church meeting. I have in mind a diaconate which seeks to serve the church meeting by giving a lead in the affairs of the church.

Team building
One of the key tasks of pastors is to spend time building their leadership team. They may not be able to build a team in the

sense of choosing their own men and women to serve with them as deacons (this is the privilege of the church meeting), but they can build the team by welding together those who have been elected to the diaconate and making them into a team. For, if the truth be told, in many of our churches the diaconate is made up of a more or less gifted group of rugged individualists, men and women doing well in their own professions and accustomed to doing their own thing at work, who then transfer the same attitudes to the diaconate. In such situations pastors need to encourage their deacons to develop their relationships with one another, and not just their relationships with their Lord. Indeed, often it is as they develop their own relationships with one another that they discover that they are enabled to develop their relationship with their Lord. The two are intertwined.

How is this process of team building best carried out?

(i) Developing a relationship with the deacons. To begin with pastors should concentrate on developing their own relationship with each of their deacons, visiting them in their own homes, listening to their hopes and aspirations, and sharing with them on an individual basis their own dreams and ideas for the church. Time spent with individual deacons and their families is never wasted. The deacons are the VIPs in the church.

(ii) Encouraging friendship among deacons. Pastors should concentrate on encouraging deacons to get to know one another outside formal deacons' meetings. The dynamics of meeting around a formal 'board' table (as is still the custom of many diaconates) are very different from relaxing with one another in one another's homes. (Incidentally, this is in itself no argument for not having formal meetings around a 'board' table. Such formal meetings can concentrate the mind wonderfully. There is no virtue in being so relaxed in the Lord's business that the meetings take twice as long to achieve half the business!) Such meetings can be

social in nature, maybe involving spouses too; or they can be highly spiritual in nature, in which deacons share with one another the things that are on their hearts.

(iii) Deacons' retreats. Team-building takes time, particularly when it is spread over a number of months. It takes time for strong men and women to allow themselves to be welded into a team, truly committed to one another. This process doesn't take just months; it can take years. For this reason some churches schedule their deacons' meetings on a fortnightly, if not a weekly, basis. However, the time commitment involved is formidable, and all the more so when one makes allowance for all the other church activities in which a deacon may be engaged.

An alternative method for short-circuiting the process of team-building is by organising occasional (say, twice a year) deacons' 'retreats' or 'away-mornings', when deacons meet away from church premises — possibly in a comfortable home where there are no young children about! — for a leisurely, long Saturday morning together (say from 8 am to 12 noon). On such occasions the normal deacons' agenda may be put to one side and time given to lengthy discussion about one or two central items of concern. Hopefully time is given to praying over such issues — and for one another too!

(iv) A weekend away. The process of team-building is above all furthered by the deacons spending a weekend away together, with or without a guest speaker for special input. This is undoubtedly a costly exercise, both in terms of finance and time, but the investment pays enormous dividends. Any diaconate is the richer for having gone away together from a Friday after work until a Sunday lunchtime. True, it means that they will be missing from a morning service, but surely any church worth its salt should be able to cope with the pastor and deacons being away for one Sunday morning!

Checking the team out

It was in fact at such a weekend that I once encouraged my deacons to embark on a spiritual checklist. It took a whole Saturday evening as we worked our way through it, first on our own, and then sharing some of our thoughts and feelings with one another. This then meant that as we gathered around the Lord's Table together the following morning, we were able to pray for one another with greater freedom and more intelligence.

A spiritual checklist for deacons

My relationship with my Lord

1. Do I find time every day for private prayer and Bible study?
2. Am I truly sorry when I confess my sins? Do I 'mourn' over them?
3. Am I growing steadily?
4. Was I ever further forward than I am now?
5. Is there an area of my life over which Jesus is not truly Lord?
6. Am I filled with the Spirit's power?
7. Am I genuinely going 'all out' for Christ?
8. Do I delight to worship Christ?
9. Am I proud?
10. Am I aware of my gifts and am I using them for the Lord?

My relationship with my family

1. What am I like at home?
2. Is there anything concerning my behaviour at home of which I would be ashamed in company?
3. Do I love, comfort, honour and protect my wife/husband?
4. Am I faithful to my wife/husband in my thoughts as well as in my life?
5. Do I pray with my wife/husband and share with her/him my deepest concerns?

6. Do I manage my children well?
7. What kind of spiritual lead do I give at home?
8. Do I have time for my family? Do I relax in their company?
9. Do I meet the needs of my parents?
10. Is our life together marked by the fruit of the Spirit?

My relationship with my fellow leaders

1. Do I pray for my pastor every day?
2. Do I encourage my pastor in the work he does?
3. Am I aware of any needs he or his family may have?
4. Is there any deacon whom I fear, dislike, criticise or hold a resentment towards?
5. Is there any deacon and his wife/her husband whom I have not welcomed to my home?
6. Is there any deacon whom I have not encouraged recently?
7. Do I keep confidences entrusted to me?
8. Am I reliable in carrying out the tasks my fellow deacons entrust to me?
9. When did I last encourage the activity leaders in the church?
10. Can my fellow deacons count on me to pray through the matters raised in earlier deacons' meetings?

My relationship with my church

1. Do I express love towards others in the fellowship?
2. Is there anybody in the fellowship I avoid?
3. Do I encourage others in the faith?
4. Am I loving enough to correct an erring brother or sister?
5. Do I make opportunities to pray with others in the fellowship?
6. Am I critical of others in the fellowship?
7. Is there anybody for whom I nourish an unforgiving spirit?
8. Do I pray for all the members of my house fellowship group?

9. Do I give generously to God's work?
10. Do I make an effort to get to know newcomers?

My relationships with 'the world'

1. Am I known as a Christian?
2. Am I seeking opportunities to build bridges of friendship with my non-Christian friends, neighbours and colleagues?
3. When did I last seek to share Christ with a friend, neighbour or colleague?
4. Am I praying for my non-Christian friends, neighbours and colleagues?
5. Do I get on with other people in general?
6. Do I always speak the truth?
7. Am I a person of the strictest honesty?
8. Do I grumble or complain constantly?
9. Do I act like 'salt' in the world?
10. Do I keep up to date with the issues affecting my neighbourhood, town, country and world?

Team training

Not only should pastors build their team, they should also train their team: ie, they should actively encourage their deacons to develop in their spiritual and theological growth. The Apostle Paul wrote to Timothy: 'The things you have heard me say in the presence of many witnesses entrust to reliable men who will also be qualified to teach others' (2 Tim 2:2). This instruction can surely be applied to the relationship between pastors and deacons. Deacons need to be trained up, so that they in turn can teach and train others. In the challenging words of George Martin:

> Perhaps pastors should imagine that they are going to have three more years in their parish as a pastor — and that there will be no replacement for them when they leave. If they acted as if this were going to happen, they would put the highest priority on selecting, motivating and training lay leaders. . . . The results of

three sustained years of such an approach would be quite significant. Even revolutionary.[1]

How can deacons be trained?

(i)   At normal deacons' meetings.   There is no reason why the first hour or so of a deacons' meeting cannot be devoted to training purposes. As I look back on my own experience of pastoral ministry, I see that there were times when we would talk about public prayer. We would talk, for instance, about the public prayer at the Lord's Table, about what precisely should be the content of the 'great prayer of thanksgiving'. We looked at the prayer that Jesus almost certainly used at the original Last Supper. We examined the content of the Eucharistic Prayer found in the Anglican *Alternative Service Book* to see if there were principles we might incorporate into our own Communion prayers. On another occasion we looked at public prayer in the context of a baptismal service and reviewed what it meant to pray for candidates immediately after their baptism. Were we simply praying that God would bless them? Or were we praying that they would be filled with the Spirit? And, if so, what exactly did we mean when we asked for such an infilling? Other concerns that we talked over included the nature of visiting applicants for church membership, and also the nature of reporting on such visits to the church meeting. We examined the nature of church membership itself; child conversion and its relationship to baptism; the various stages of spiritual development as far as young people are concerned; charismatic renewal and restorationism; the third world and the missionary challenge; the role of deacons, etc.

(ii)   Reading material.   A second form of training is to feed the minds of deacons with good books and magazines. Pastors can ensure that their deacons are reading and thinking by giving them copies of books and articles that have stimulated them. Yes, magazine articles can be photocopied,

books lent, and occasionally books even purchased. (I remember once how I was so impressed with a particular book that I bought a copy for all fourteen deacons, and then put the cost down on church expenses!)

(iii) Courses and conferences. A third form of training is actually to send deacons away on courses or conferences. On a less formal level, training of a kind can be carried out by sending deacons to visit churches which have been particularly successful in one area or another of Christian life and mission. It is so easy for deacons to become narrow-minded and unaware of what God is doing beyond their own borders. Not that there is any point in simply taking over somebody else's ideas. But sometimes there is much to be said for adapting (as distinct from 'adopting') what one church is doing to one's own.

Team responsibilities

What exactly are the responsibilities of a diaconate? In a leaflet I wrote for the Baptist Basics Series, entitled *The Ministry of Deacons* (Baptist Union: London), I defined the ministry of a deacon in five main categories.

(i) The care of the fellowship. Along with the minister, the deacons are responsible for the pastoral care of the church. Deacons can care by:

(a) developing a system of pastoral care whereby all the members and friends of the church are 'covered'. In many churches the membership is split between the deacons, with each deacon being responsible for a specific number of families or individuals in the church. In other churches pastoral care is exercised through house groups run by deacons.

(b) accompanying the pastor on certain of his visits. When he gives Communion to a housebound member, he will want one or two deacons to be there to represent the church. When asked to pray for the healing of a sick member, he may wish, on the basis of James 5, to take several deacons along with him to the house.

(c) getting to know all the members of the church. Names are important. To remember a person's name is to show we care for them (see John 10:3). Aim to get to know at least one new name a week.

(d) welcoming visitors to the church. In many churches deacons form a 'door-duty' rota. However, a warm handshake is not enough. After service be prepared to talk to newcomers and, where appropriate, welcome them back to your home.

(e) visiting applicants for membership. In most Baptist churches, deacons — often alongside a non-deacon member — visit those applying for membership. This is a solemn responsibility and should never be rushed. The visit will provide an opportunity to hear about the applicant's spiritual experience, to remind him/her of the responsibilities of church membership, and generally to extend a hand of friendship to them. After such a visit a bond will normally have been formed between the visitor and the applicant. In many churches the deacon is then responsible for keeping an eye on the new member, giving encouragement and help where necessary.

(ii) Leadership in worship and teaching. The pastor is primarily responsible for the worship and teaching of the church. But deacons may share in this ministry. In the major worship services of the church, deacons may serve in a number of ways:

(a) serving at the Lord's Table. In all Baptist churches deacons help in the serving of the bread and the wine.

(b) praying at the Lord's Table. In many Baptist churches deacons lead in the prayer of thanksgiving for the bread and the wine. This is no small responsibility. It is wise to come prepared. Some find it helpful to find out the theme of the pastor's sermon the day before so that their prayer can neatly dovetail. Above all, it is important to centre the prayer on praise and thanksgiving for the Lord Jesus.

(c)   leadership in worship. In this country deacons with the right gifts are sharing more and more in the leading of public worship. The variety of approach is appreciated by pastor and people alike.

(d)   leadership in small groups. Small-group activity is common to the life of most of our churches. In many churches deacons are the natural leaders for such groups.

(iii)   The care of the pastor.   Deacons also have a special 'ministry' towards their pastor. As in Acts 6, today's deacons should free their minister to fulfil his ministry. But even more than that, they should care for him as a person and give him all the support he needs.

  Deacons will care:

(a)   by giving encouragement. Pastors are human. They need encouragement, particularly after they have given of themselves in the preaching of the word, but also at other times.

(b)   by prayer. Deacons, like other members, are able to pray daily for their pastor. But deacons also have a special opportunity to pray with — and for — their pastor in the vestry.

(c)   by providing opportunities for study. This is one sure way of guaranteeing freshness and depth in the pastor's ministry. A minister's time in his study should be respected and not trespassed on, except in emergencies. Many churches encourage their pastor to read by giving him a generous book allowance. An annual study-leave of a week or two will benefit the church. So also the three months' sabbatical which Baptist ministers are encouraged to take every eight years.

(d)   by seeing that he has an adequate salary. 'The labourer deserves his wages' (Lk 10:7; 1 Tim 5:17). This will work to the advantage of the church: for freed from money worries and from the possible necessity of 'moonlighting', the pastor will be able to give himself more to his ministry.

(e) by ensuring he has some time off. Does your pastor take a day off? Does everybody in the church know what day he has off? Do your pastor and his family take a proper annual holiday? Your pastor can only fulfil his ministry effectively if he is fresh in the Lord's service.

(f) by providing secretarial assistance. No pastor is called to be an office clerk, yet many ministers spend hours writing letters, duplicating notes and sorting out a variety of administrative tasks. Secretarial assistance — even if it be limited — is essential. So also is office equipment.

(iv) Participation in the deacons' meeting. There is much to be said for circulating the agenda on the Sunday before the deacons' meeting. In this way all the deacons can come to the meeting prayerfully prepared.

(v) Leadership in the church meeting. Deacons should not be afraid to speak at the church meeting, for they, too, are members. Particularly when a deacons' recommendation is brought to the church meeting, it is often helpful for a number of deacons to speak in its support. Hopefully, the recommendation will be unanimous: however, if a deacon dissents from the consensus view of the diaconate, he is at liberty, having first given due warning to his colleagues, to explain his point of view in the church meeting. The church meeting has appointed deacons from its midst, and in doing so has entrusted them with authority. Yes, of course, the deacons are ultimately subject to the church meeting: but the service of deacons is to lead. Deacons should not be afraid to exercise this leadership. True, the church meeting should not be a rubber stamp of the deacons' meeting. On the other hand, where there is a unanimous recommendation, it should only be rejected by the church meeting on the strongest of grounds (see Heb 13:7).

Apart from what now might be perceived as 'sexist' language (the pastor throughout this document was referred to as 'he'), I would still stand by this as an example of team responsibilities within the church.

The ideal team

But is there in fact a definitive list of deacons' responsibilities? On one occasion I played an interesting game with my deacons and their spouses. Towards the end of a social evening together, I distributed the following list and asked them to list in order of priority what they felt our diaconate should ideally be doing.

1. *Visiting*. Calling on members in their homes: eg, the sick, the widowed, members of one's fellowship group, etc.
2. *Leading in public prayer*. At the Communion Table, but also taking an active role in prayer meetings of all kinds.
3. *Counselling*. As 'elder'(!) statesmen, counselling individuals on personal and spiritual problems.
4. *Teaching*. Involvement not only in leading fellowship groups, but also in (specialist) groups such as Searchers, Starters and Stretchers.
5. *Supporting activity leaders*. Taking an active interest in the Sunday school and other organisations. Listening to the leaders and encouraging them in their work.
6. *Leadership*. Seeing visions and dreaming dreams; producing ideas and showing initiative; setting the pace with the pastor.
7. *Administration*. A management team, looking after the day-to-day business of the church, freeing the minister for ministry.
8. *Supporting members in 'full-time' service*. Not leaving ongoing support to particular interest groups, but taking a special responsibility for those we have set apart.
9. *Practical service*. Seeing to the practical needs of the building and of the fellowship — 'doers'.
10. *Representation*. Representing the various age and interest groups in the church, so that the diaconate automatically has the finger on the pulse of the church.

11. *Interviewing.* Interviewing people for membership, and then maintaining an ongoing pastoral brief for them.
12. *Wider church responsibilities.* Representing the church on various ecumenical and denominational committees.
13. *Caring for the minister and his family.* Exercising pastoral care for a family which otherwise might not be cared for.

As I later indicated to my deacons and their spouses, there were in fact two 'catches' in this questionnaire.

First of all, the list omitted the priority of 'being': being on the one hand a man or woman of God, and on the other hand being men and women of God together. As Bruce Larson has written:

> Your leadership in the church will be felt more by how we live together and model authentic life than by the decisions we make about budget and staff and programme. We're not just a board of directors. We're here as the elected, ordained leaders of this church, and they trust us to *be* something together.[2]

Secondly, leadership apart, there is no one list of priorities for any given diaconate, just as there is certainly no one list of priorities for any given deacon. Woe betide a diaconate if only some of the functions on the above list are not present. All are needed. What's more, woe betide a diaconate if all the deacons are gifted in the same area; if all, for instance, are super at caring for the pastor, but no good at practical service. A diaconate needs to be multi-gifted. It needs to have on it men and women of varying gifting.

Team meetings

A whole host of practical questions arises in relation to deacons' meetings and a leader needs to sort out:

(1) *How frequently* a diaconate should meet. I have already made clear earlier my hesitation about deacons meeting too frequently. Unless a church is going through a

period of crisis there seems no good reason why a diaconate should meet as a diaconate more than once a month. It may well be that sub-committees might meet in between time — but not the diaconate as such.

(2) *The length* of the deacons' meetings. This should be limited. All too often one hears horror stories of deacons' meetings going on until midnight. Again, unless there is a particular crisis, there is no reason for such long meetings — it is simply ill discipline. With good chairmanship and good organisation a deacons' meeting should be able to do its business in three hours or less. This should also include any time set aside for 'training'.

(3) *The chairmanship* of the deacons' meeting. In Britain this is normally in the hands of the pastor. Interestingly, in the USA it is often in the hands of one of the deacons. For my part I see chairmanship as being part of the pastor's leadership role — as chairman (helmsman) the pastor is actively guiding and encouraging the meeting along.

(4) *The drawing up of the agenda*. This is too important a matter simply to be delegated. An agenda reflects the spiritual priorities of a church. In too many churches the top three items on a deacons' agenda are (i) finance, (ii) fabric, (iii) correspondence. Such agendas are surely the death-knell to the church. Items such as membership (baptisms, transfers, etc) and mission should come at the top. Furthermore, the whole meeting should be laced with prayer. It is not sufficient to have prayer at the beginning, for at that stage the substance of many an item is still unknown. Nor is it sufficient to have prayer at the end, for by that time many a deacon is too tired to pray in a concentrated and adequate fashion. There is a lot to be said for having a prayer slot half way through the meeting — and for feeling free to encourage prayer at any point which seems particularly appropriate.

Renewing the team

From time to time there are deacons' elections. In most churches deacons are elected to serve for three years, with an option to serve a further term of service. In some churches there is a limit to the number of times a deacon may serve consecutively. In such cases deacons have to take a 'sabbatical' and stand down for a year after, say, two terms of service. Where there is a glut of leadership potential, there may be something to be said for this practice.

One question which is not always considered is this: is a deacons' election always an election? If a deacon is being returned for yet another period of service, the term 'election' does not seem the most appropriate. Might we perhaps not speak of deacons in such cases being confirmed to their particular office or ministry within the church?

As for those who are being nominated for the first time, there is a lot to be said for the pastor meeting with them and ensuring that the candidates understand for what exactly they are allowing their names to go forward. Indeed, in my experience many people who are approached for office often come in the first place to the pastor to talk things through before allowing their name to go forward. Certainly, once deacons are elected, it is helpful to spell out in very practical terms what precisely is involved. An annual running through responsibilities does no harm — not even for long-serving deacons.

2. Teams within the team

So far I may have given the impression that there may only be one team within the team. In fact there may be a whole number of leadership teams within the overall team (ie, the church).

Elders and deacons

In Baptist life there has been no one pattern of shared leadership. John Smyth, who organised the first English Baptist church in Amsterdam at the beginning of the seventeenth century, in his last confession defined the church as having two sorts of 'ministers':

> Christ hath set in His outward church two sorts of ministers: viz, some who are called pastors, teachers, or elders, who administer the word and sacraments, and others, who are called deacons, men and women: whose ministry is to serve tables and wash the saints' feet.[3]

Smyth was not here referring to the church in general, but to the local church. Within any given local church he envisaged there being elders and deacons. Increasingly, however, the eldership was identified with a one-man ministry, with the result that today most English Baptist churches have simply a pastor and a board (sometimes quaintly called a 'court'!) of deacons.

Church life, however, never stands still. Today an increasing number of Baptist churches are adopting the pattern of elders and deacons again. This is done not on the grounds of being true to Baptist tradition(!), but rather of being true to the Scriptures. *The* scriptural pattern of leadership, it is argued, is elders and deacons. But is this in fact so?

Clearly this was the pattern of ministry operating in the churches of Ephesus for which Timothy was responsible (see 1 Timothy 3:1–13), but it does not necessarily appear to have been the universal pattern. This should not be surprising, in so far as it is clear that there was never one blue-print for ministry in New Testament times. The church at Jerusalem was structured differently from the church at Corinth, and almost certainly the church at Corinth was structured differently from the church at Ephesus. This being so, care should be taken in advancing the claim that the pattern of elders and deacons is laid down in Scripture as the model for church life. It is not. It is just one model.

To complicate matters, we have no sure knowledge of the precise role which deacons played over against elders in the Ephesian church. Thus Paul in 1 Timothy 3:8–13 is far more interested in the qualities necessary for deacons as distinct from the duties expected of deacons. There are those who equate the deacons of 1 Timothy 3 with the seven men 'known to be full of the Spirit and wisdom' who in Acts 6:1–6 were chosen 'to wait (*diakonein*) on tables'. But such an equation is highly unlikely. The seven did not form the kind of management team responsible for such mundane matters of church life such as finance and fabric, which seems to be the role of deacons in churches which have elders and deacons. Rather, they had a key role to play in the pastoral care of the widows of Jerusalem. As Luke develops the story of the church in Acts, it becomes clear that these seven were spiritual leaders of the kind of standing which is normally accorded to elders today.

But to revert to the pattern now being adopted in many churches: the elders are seen as having a leadership role in the spiritual and pastoral affairs of the church, while the deacons are seen as responsible for the more practical aspects of the church's life. On this model, the pastor is one of the elders — normally the 'presiding' elder. In principle there is no reason why this pattern of ministry cannot be happily adopted in the life of a church. In practice, however, it does not always prove ideal. Thus the distinction between the 'spiritual' and the 'practical' cannot easily be maintained — the handling of money, for instance, normally seen as a diaconal responsibility, calls for a high degree of spirituality. Many a pastor has reason to thank God for a godly church treasurer, endued with the spiritual gift of wisdom!

Secondly, the almost inevitable distinction between 'first' and 'second-class' leaders is not helpful. Whatever the theory, in practice churches perceive a clear distinction in status between elders and deacons, for the simple reason that one group is apparently more 'spiritual' than another!

Thirdly, there is a tendency, brought about by the fact that pastors often nominate their own elders, for elders to be in the same mould as the pastor. The result is that elders sometimes fail to complement their pastor. Phil Greenslade, admittedly in a different context, pertinently quotes Charles Blair: 'Are your co-workers a completion of yourself? Or simply an extension? If I am called to leadership and find helpers who are simply echoes of myself, I double my strengths but I also double my weaknesses.'[4] My observation is that, unlike deacons (of whom there are normally more), elders tend to be duplicates of their pastors. Those churches that operate with such a pattern of ministry need to take great care that they do not fall into this trap.

On a different note, I confess I find it hard to understand the popularity of the term 'elder'. It is, of course, scriptural, but that doesn't necessarily prove that the term is normative today. Wearing veils is scriptural, but on the whole most ladies in our churches don't wear them, for the simple reason that veils are a phenomenon of a past culture. The same is true of elders. In the first-century world, be it predominantly Greek, Roman or Jewish, people were either 'young' or 'old'. Thus in Roman society a man was called a *iuvenis* (a young man) when he was under forty, and a *senex* (an old man) when he was forty or over. There was no such thing as middle-age. Yet in our churches today there are plenty of middle-aged men who are dignified with the title 'old man' (ie, elder) — a strange phenomenon indeed!

An alternative to the elders and deacons model, which obviates some of the difficulties we have mentioned, would be to have a diaconate which included a sub-committee (an administration team) responsible for the day-to-day running of the church's affairs, with particular regard to such matters as finance, fabric and administration. This in effect frees the deacons' meeting to concentrate on the more strategic and pastoral affairs of the church, without anybody being perceived as having been 'demoted' or 'aged'. In effect, on this model deacons adopt the role of 'elders'.

Ultimately, of course, names for leaders are irrelevant. What matters is that the functions of leadership are present, and in particular that the leadership that is exercised is shared. This principle is to be found in all the models we have examined in this section.

Multi-directional ministry teams

Yet another model of leadership teams within the overall team (ie, the church) is possible: multi-directional ministry. Here I have in mind, in particular, the creation of ministry teams responsible for the main areas of the church's mission. This model of ministry is described in detail in the book I co-authored with Alan Wilkinson, *Turning the Tide*. In summary, we developed the idea of setting up multi-directional, task-orientated ministry teams where leadership gifts could more easily be released. In practice, this meant that in the church at Altrincham we developed five ministry teams.

(i) A *Social Action Team* sought to identify and meet the social needs of the community. It was responsible for various 'task forces' and constantly prodded people to get involved.

(ii) An *Evangelism Team* sought to encourage the church to 'by all means save some'. It was responsible for initiating new evangelistic projects and encouraging current evangelistic activities.

(iii) A *Nurturing Team* was in the business of seeing people built up in their faith, and was particularly responsible for all the church's small group activity. It devised study programmes, selected leaders, and called leaders together to talk through the progress — or lack of progress — that their groups were making.

(iv) A *Development Team* built on the work of the Nurturing Team and sought to draw out people's natural and spiritual gifts so that they could be used to greatest effect within the body. This team was also responsible for thinking through matters relating to the ongoing development of the life of the church as a whole, and bringing any appropriate proposals to the deacons' meeting.

(v) A *Pastoral Team* co-ordinated the wider work of visiting, and shared with the pastor the workload of counselling and general pastoring.[5]

It is important to note that these five ministry teams were compact in size. They were responsible for thinking and praying through possible courses of action, but did not necessarily do all the work themselves. They simply sought to spearhead the work and encouraged others to get stuck in.

Another important fact to note is that, unlike the deacons' meeting of which the pastor, as 'senior partner', was chairman, these ministry teams were each headed up by a different deacon. This was more than a fancy detail. Psychologically it made an enormous difference. For then the deacons — and not the pastor — had to take the initiative in drawing up the agenda and seeing that decisions were carried out. In other words, gifts for leadership were released.

It is a sad fact that frequently the larger a church is, the more difficult it becomes for 'lay' people to lead. The temptation is to add full-time members of staff to do the work of the 'laity'. This particular multi-directional task-orientated model overcomes some of these problems. It releases gifts for leadership. It helps to ensure that when extra members are added to the full-time team, then their business is seen to be to a large extent that of equipping and enabling others to fulfil their 'ministries' rather than seeking to replace them.

Clearly the model that I have just described operated within a particular church at a particular time. The beauty of it, however, is that in principle it did not need to be restricted to a particular place and a particular time. It is easily adapted to very different situations. Thus in a small church it might not be appropriate to consider operating five teams — indeed, the church might be so small that initially the idea of having more than one leadership team at all might seem impossible. The model, however, would allow a pastor to ask two of his deacons to share in the overall leadership of the church — one could be responsible for all that took place within the evangelising sector of church life, and the other might be responsible for all that took place on the nurturing side of church life. Responsibilities would be shared — furthermore, responsibilities could be shared in such a way that the church could maintain a balanced all-round ministry.

Problems of team leadership

Elsewhere I have written of the joys and strengths of team leadership. There can, however, be problems too. Personality clashes, misunderstandings and relationship difficulties are bound to happen for the simple reason that these teams are made up of fallible men and women. In the words of John Blattner:

> It seems to be an immutable fact that 'wherever two or three are gathered in Jesus' name', sooner or later there are going to be people problems. This is just as true among leaders as among other folks. We needn't be surprised. Galatians 5:20–21 makes it clear that discord, jealousy, ambition, dissension, factionalism and all the rest, are part of the fallen human nature that pastoral leaders share with everyone else. Occasional problems among leaders are inevitable, given what leaders are made of.[6]

Accordingly, good leaders would be wise to face up to ways of resolving possible tension and conflict long before it actually appears.

In this area John Tiller and Mark Birchall have some good advice to offer. In particular they offer five positive approaches to resolving conflict.

(1) *Recognise that some conflict is natural.* It has been suggested that in teams (as in marriages) where there is no conflict at all, 'either the team do not know each other very well or they do not interact very much'.

(2) *Identify the real cause of the conflict.* A useful course of action here is to bring in an outside 'consultant' (eg, an Area Superintendent, an archdeacon, an 'apostle').

(3) *Recognise that right attitudes are essential.* Dare we ask, 'My brother/sister, have I said or done anything that has hurt you?' It is never easy, but it may be vital.

(4) *Recognise the need for varied gifts*. Humility means recognising and valuing the gifts of other members of the team — the pastor doesn't necessarily know it all!

(5) *Establish an agreed decision-making process*. What happens if the pastor disagrees with most if not all of the rest of the team? The simplest answer is to recognise that the pastor has the final say![7]

The above is but a summary of the advice that Birchall and Tiller have to offer as a result of extensive research into the way in which leadership teams operate in churches today. One problem, however, which Birchall and Tiller did not deal with specifically is what happens when there are problems among or differences between full-time members of the leadership team: eg, pastors and associate pastors. Clearly, given that all of us are of 'flesh and blood', then such problems are inevitable. Therefore they need to be anticipated. All too often churches seem to lack structures to deal with the niggles which, left to themselves, can turn sour and develop into deep divisions. Some kind of regular 'support group' is necessary. Most diaconates are far too large to deal with matters of this kind — the confidentiality and intimacy of a small group of two or three people (the 'full-timers' apart) is necessary. Some elderships might fulfil this function. Otherwise there is much to be said for forming a support group to meet specifically and regularly for the purpose of nipping problems in the bud. Preventative care is always better than curative care.

3. Setting the team(s) to work

So far in our discussion I have assumed that the pastor will be happy to delegate. Indeed, implicit in the idea of shared leadership is the principle of delegation. No pastor can successfully go it alone. In theological and practical terms one-man/one-woman ministry is a nonsense.

Alas, 'nonsense' continues to be practised in many a

quarter. Michael Griffiths describes the sorry situation in somewhat graphic terms:

> The 'ordained ministry' seems a great hindrance to church growth, because it is supported by the 'collusion in dependence' between one-man-band individualists who would like to run everything themselves, and lazy congregations who would rather delegate everything to the dedicated professional. But how can we win the race when ministers would rather teach themselves, than teach faithful persons who will then teach others also? It is as though the first runner in a relay refuses to pass on the baton, but insists on attempting to run the whole distance solo. Motivation for church growth will be encouraged if it is not fettered to a pre-Gutenberg ecclesiology centring on parson and squire.[8]

Sharing the load

It has been said, 'It is better to set ten men to work than to do the work of ten men, even if one is able to do so' (a statement variously attributed to DL Moody and John Mott!). In fact, no one can do the work of ten men. This is the reason why all too often the pastor is the 'cork in the bottle': he holds on to the reins too much.

Pastors need to learn to use their good people. Andrew Carnegie, the great industrialist of the late nineteenth and early twentieth century, was once asked the secret of his success: 'Always having people around me who are smarter than I am,' was his reply. Alas some pastors are so insecure that they feel threatened by those who are more gifted than they.

Delegation, of course, is no modern principle. The 'patron saint of all management consultants' is in fact an Old Testament character, Jethro. Thus in Exodus 18 we read that when Jethro went to visit his son-in-law, Moses, he saw immediately that Moses was carrying too much responsibility on his shoulders. 'What is this you are doing for the people? Why do you alone sit as judge, while all these people stand round you from morning to evening? . . . What you are doing is not good. You and these people who come to you will only wear yourselves out. The work is too heavy for you; you cannot handle it alone' (Ex 18:14, 17–18). Jethro then proposed that Moses should continue to act as God's representative, responsible for the teaching of spiritual principles and exercising his legalistic functions, but that he should delegate other areas of judicial responsibility to competent men. By doing this Moses could concentrate on the more important aspects of his leadership, at the same time making it possible for others to share responsibility and be trained in the art of leadership.

Ron Trudinger has done some arithmetic on Exodus 18, linking it with Exodus 38:26 where the number of men 'twenty years old or more' is said to be 603,550. On the basis of this population figure, Trudinger reasons that Moses would have needed 600 leaders of 'thousands', 6,000 leaders of 'hundreds', 12,000 leaders of 'fifties', and 60,000 leaders of 'tens'. This makes a total of 78,600 people whom Moses involved in leadership![9]

The biblical principle of delegation is also seen in Acts 6. There we read how the Apostles delegated the care of the widows to the seven 'deacons'. Thereupon, Luke tells us, 'the word of God spread. The number of disciples in Jerusalem increased rapidly' (Acts 6:7). The clear implication is that when the Apostles delegated their work, the church began to grow.

In 1979 Lewis Misselbrook, then of the Baptist Union Department of Mission, made a study of six growing churches in California. In his unpublished paper he wrote that all six churches shared one common factor: 'they all believed in multiple leadership ... and counted the one-man ministry as unbiblical and unproductive unless a church wishes to remain small'. A sobering thought.

Delegation is therefore clearly an essential mark of a leader who desires to see his church grow. In this respect an epitaph once produced by Montgomery is pertinent: 'Here lies one who died of exhaustion brought about by preoccupation with detail. He never had time to think.'[10] There is a limit to what one person can achieve. In a growing situation people will either drive themselves into the ground or stunt the church's growth, unless they are prepared to delegate.

Why pastors fail to delegate

Ted Engstrom lists five searching reasons as to why Christian leaders won't delegate.

(1) They believe that subordinates won't be able to handle the assignment.

(2) They fear competition from subordinates.

(3) They are afraid of losing recognition.

(4) They are fearful that their weaknesses will be exposed.

(5) They feel that they won't have the time to turn over the work and provide the necessary training.[11]

None of these reasons reflect creditably on pastoral ministry. They emphasise rather the insecurity felt by so many pastors. Here is a challenge to theological educators!

Defining responsibility

So far I have talked of delegation, but not in fact defined our terms. A useful definition is that made by LA Allen, and cited with approval by Olan Hendrix: 'Delegation is entrusting *responsibility* and *authority* and establishing lines of *accountability*.'[12]

Ted Engstrom elaborates in more detail on what he terms the four basic ideas of delegation.

(1) *Transfer of work*. An assigned task goes from the leader to subordinate, and the subordinate accepts the delegated work on the basis of the expected results.

(2) *Transfer of authority*. This is essential in most cases. Most experts in management and organisation feel that authority should be commensurate with the nature of the work.

(3) *Acceptance of responsibility*. If delegation is to be effective, the subordinate must be genuinely willing

to perform the work and must have the initiative to get it done.

(4) *Importance of follow-up and accountability*. Delegation does not mean abandoning all interest in the work. The leader is still accountable, and therefore he should always be available and ready to give the subordinate help or advice if and when he needs it.[13]

No doubt all these points are important. For my part I would emphasise the importance of accountability. Delegation is not the same as abdication. Shared leadership does not involve a total letting go of the reins. There must always be an element of reporting back. It has been said, 'people do what we *inspect*, not what we *expect*.' That is true, even within Christian circles.

Living by priorities

How, then, should we delegate? David Cormack provides some helpful rules for delegation.

(1) Provide complete information on the task. What is the target? When is it to be completed? What standards are you expecting?

(2) Define precisely the limits of responsibility of the person in relation to the task. Satisfy yourself that he understands them: eg, how much money can be spent, what equipment can be used, to whom can he talk?

(3) Don't provide the answers, but help the person to find them. Where might he look for information, guidance, etc?

(4) Don't make the decisions for the person — give him as much freedom as you can.

(5) Don't be hasty in criticising mistakes. You might not have made the same mistake, but you might have made another.

(6) Follow up on delegation. Agree when you will check to see that progress is being made.

(7) Encourage the initiative of the other person so that he can cope with emergencies if they arise, rather than running back to you.

(8) Never publicly countermand a decision taken by the person to whom you have delegated. Allow him to reverse it.

(9) Back up your people to the limit that your conscience will allow.

(10) Accept responsibility for all decisions that you delegate.[14]

To Cormack's ten rules for delegation, I would add an eleventh — although in fact it may be regarded as an expansion of the seventh: never be chary in allotting praise where it is due. Just as people need to be corrected when they have done wrong, so too they need to be praised when they have done well. In this connection, Lord Montgomery tells a story told him by Sir Winston Churchill concerning the Duke of Wellington in his last years. A friend asked him, 'If you had your life over again, is there any way in which you could have done better?' The old duke replied, 'Yes, I should have given more praise.'[15] Here is a lesson for any leader.

Delegation is essential if a leader is to be effective in achieving the task. Delegation is the only way possible for a leader to work with others. Initially, of course, it can take extra time to delegate, to train, to instruct in a job. It always takes longer to show someone how to do something than to do it oneself. But as Andrew Le Peau rightly maintains, 'Failure to delegate because of this is almost always a failure to live by priorities. It keeps you bogged down in details and prevents you from taking the necessary periodic looks at the big picture.'[16] Delegation is the mark of a leader.

Notes

1. George Martin, quoted by David Watson, *Discipleship* (Hodder and Stoughton: London, 1981), p 80.
2. Bruce Larson, 'None of us are sinners', *Leadership*, vol 5, no 4 (autumn 1984), pp 12–23.
3. Quoted by EA Payne, *The Fellowship of Believers*

4. Philip Greenslade, *Leadership* (Marshalls: Basingstoke, 1984), p 76.
5. Paul Beasley-Murray and Alan Wilkinson, *Turning the Tide* (Bible Society: London, 1981), pp 73–78.
6. John Blattner, 'People Problems among Leaders', *Pastoral Renewal*, vol 11, no 7 (February 1987).
7. John Tiller with Mark Birchall, *The Gospel Community and its Leadership* (Marshall Pickering: Basingstoke, 1987), pp 117–125.
8. Michael Griffiths, 'Evangelism and Church Planting — Future Directions for Church Growth', in Monica Hill, ed, *How to Plant Churches* (MARC: Bromley, 1984), p 131.
9. Ron Trudinger, *Cells for Life* (Olive Tree Publications: Basingstoke, 1979), pp 25–26.
10. Quoted by Michael Saward, *All Change* (Hodder and Stoughton: London, 1983), p 84.
11. Ted Engstrom, *The Making of a Christian Leader* (Zondervan: Grand Rapids, MI, 1976), p 164.
12. Olan Hendrix, *Management for the Christian Worker* (Quill Publications: Santa Barbara, CA, 1976), p 83.
13. Ted Engstrom, *op cit*, p 163.
14. David Cormack, *Team Spirit* (MARC: Bromley, 1987), pp 61–62.
15. Lord Montgomery, *The History of Warfare* (Collins: London).
16. Andrew Le Peau, *Paths of Leadership* (Scripture Union: London, 1984), p 66.

8

Leadership in Action: the Team Members

We return to our definition: the good leader works as a senior partner with other members to achieve the task, build the team, and meet individual needs. From the task and the team, we now turn to the individual team members, the individual members of the church. They have a variety of needs. It is the task of the leader to ensure that those needs are met.

What are those needs? It seems to me that they are fivefold. Individuals need:
— to be led in worship
— to be taught
— to receive pastoral care
— to experience fellowship
— to find avenues of service.

1. Worship

People have 'worship' needs in the sense that their very being cries out to worship God. Worship is not an optional extra, but an essential part of life. Indeed, worship is life. As David Owen once put it: 'It is as natural for man to worship as it is for him to breathe.'[1] 'The one essential condition of human existence,' wrote Dostoievsky, 'is that man should always be able to bow down to something infinitely great.'

For the Christian that 'something infinitely great' is, of course, 'the God and Father of our Lord Jesus Christ'. 'Praise be to the God and Father of our Lord Jesus Christ,' exclaimed the Apostle Paul, 'who has blessed us in the heavenly realms with every spiritual blessing in Christ' (Eph 1:3). It is this note of praise that wells up in the heart of every individual Christian believer.

The task of the leader is to give opportunity to God's people to express their praise. More than that, it is the task of a leader to give direction to God's people's praises. To enable them so to look on God, that they will be lost in 'wonder, love and praise'.

Giving God the glory

Leading worship is an art — and also a science. The worship leader is far more than a 'master of ceremonies' whose job it is to ensure that things flow smoothly and that everybody has a good time. Leading worship involves leading people into the presence of God. For this to happen worship must be God-centred and not man-centred. The emphasis is not on our feelings, but on God's 'worthiness'.

Many helpful definitions of worship have been given. A memorable one was given by William Temple:

> Worship is the submission of all our nature to God. It is the quickening of conscience by his holiness; the nourishment of mind with his truth; the purifying of imagination by his beauty; the opening of the heart to his love; the surrender of will to his purpose — and all of this gathered up in adoration, the most selfless emotion of which our nature is capable, and therefore the chief remedy for that self-centredness which is our original sin and the source of all our actual sin.[2]

Similarly, David Owen writes:

> True worship is looking upon God, concentrating our whole beings — minds, eyes, ears, emotions, wills — upon his presence,

thereby offering him our best and laying ourselves open to his transforming grace. 'We all . . . beholding the glory of the Lord,' said Paul, 'are being changed into his likeness' (2 Cor 3:18, RSV). That is worship.[3]

Personally, I like the definition offered by Ralph Martin: 'Worship is the dramatic celebration of God in his supreme worth in such a manner that his "worthiness" becomes the norm and inspiration of human living.'[4] Rightly understood, the emphasis in worship is on 'giving God the glory'. Indeed, our very English word 'worship' derives from the Saxon *weorthscipe* which became 'worthship'. In worship we acknowledge God's worth. We give him the glory by telling him how he actually is. As the psalmist put it, we 'ascribe to the Lord the glory due to his name' (Ps 29:2).

It is this kind of worship which the human heart desires. Worship where God is at the centre. 'As the deer pants for streams of water, so my soul pants for you, O God' (Ps 42:1). The psalmist's experience is common to all of us, yet how frequently we are disappointed. The words of the Methodist, Donald English, are even more true today than when they were first written: 'The fact seems to be that our Christian description of worship at its best, and our Christian experience of worship as we currently know it, are rather far removed from one another.'[5]

Losing direction

What has gone wrong?

First of all, in many circles worship has become man-centred. The emphasis is on our feelings. We spend much of our time telling God how we feel, as an examination of any collection of modern songs quickly reveals. Furthermore, there is a tendency to expect that worship should always make us feel good. Instead of coming to worship God because he is God, we come to worship God because we need a boost. 'Join us for worship,' declared a notice-board outside a church, 'you will feel better for it.' But is that necessarily true? If God is to the fore, we may not initially feel better at all. An encounter with God may actually prove to be painful and may entail a call to sacrifice, commitment and self-denial. In the words of Ralph Martin: 'The call is not so much "Smile, God loves you", as "Repent", "Weep", "Tremble".'[6]

Secondly, much contemporary evangelical worship has lost its sense of direction. The sense of movement implicit in some of the traditional orders of service has been abandoned, and little of substance has been put in their place. Don't get me wrong. I have no doubt that the old 'hymn-sandwich', into which the traditional Reformed order of service degenerated, has had its day. I delight in the movement of charismatic renewal which has swept through so many of our churches, bringing with it a fresh understanding of worship and a fresh desire to worship God. How much poorer contemporary worship would be without the new songs. God has indeed poured out his Spirit on his people in a new way. But the 'new wine' of his Spirit is heady stuff. It has burst its old containers. It needs new wine-skins, new worship structures, if it is to be contained.

Alas, in many free and independent evangelical churches, there are no structures. Worship for the most part lacks form and therefore lacks direction. Many pastors have abdicated their traditional role of leading worship and handed it over to the church's musicians, without apparently realising that there is a great difference between leading songs and leading worship.

If worship is to be truly satisfying, if worship is to lead into the presence of God, if worship is to provide the norms and inspiration for living, then there must be structure and direction. Freedom without form all too often means that worship becomes a man-centred emotional experience which does not actually meet the needs of the heart. In other words, even in non-liturgical churches, the worship leader needs to have a sense of liturgy. The task of the pastor is to ensure that there is a sense of liturgy. Pastors may not always lead the worship. Nonetheless they are responsible for the overall direction of the worship. It is for this that they have been trained. Leading worship is both an art and a science.

It is precisely because the emphasis in much worship has been on an experience rather than on God that it has become increasingly rare to focus on the holiness of God. The result is that in many evangelical churches prayers of confession have fallen into disuse. In the average evangelical free church, strange to say, we no longer confess our sins. Yet the human heart longs to start afresh with God. Even in non-priestly circles, there is many a burdened sinner who longs to hear God declare a word of absolution. But no: this need is unmet.

Many a concerned Christian longs to bring the needs of the world before God in public worship. But again, precisely because the emphasis is upon 'us' and our feelings, the world and its needs are passed by. By and large in evangelical churches prayers of intercession do not feature. Or if they do, then such prayers are for the members of the fellowship who are in need. The concerns of the wider world are neglected. The Christian duty to pray for kings and all those in positions of authority (1 Tim 2:1–2) is forgotten.

Possibly linked to this emphasis on 'us' is the current desire no longer to listen to God's voice speaking to his people. Strange as it may sound, the reading of God's word is being pushed aside in many evangelical churches. Indeed, the more Bible-believing the church apparently is, the less likelihood there is of hearing Scripture read. In the average Baptist church, it is rare for there to be two 'lessons' in any given service — a few verses from one passage of Scripture normally suffice. The result is that the members of the congregation are deprived.

Do I caricature? I don't think so. As one who travels the country Sunday by Sunday, I know. Time and again before being called on to preach, I sit in the pew being led in a form of worship which fails to satisfy. I dare to believe that I am not the only dissatisfied customer. God's people are suffering. They are suffering for lack of good leadership. The wise pastor will indeed ensure that the worship needs of all God's people are met.

Getting back on track

If the worship needs of God's people are to be met, we need to follow these simple remedies.

(1) *Shape and direction needs to be given to services of worship.* Worship doesn't just happen, it needs to be led. Structure is necessary even for the most 'open' of services. Yes, even a charismatic 'free-for-all', where contributions are invited from the worshipping congregation, benefits from structure — so that, for instance, praise leads to proclamation, and proclamation then leads to prayer.

Structure and direction do not negate the working of the Spirit. Indeed, the reverse is often true. For just as the Spirit inspired order within Scripture, so he inspires order within worship. 'Everything should be done in a fitting and orderly way' (1 Cor 14:40) wrote Paul. The freedom of the Spirit is no mandate for human disorganisation.

(2) *God should be given the glory in worship.* Care needs to be exercised in the choice of hymns and songs, to ensure that the focus is on God. Likewise prayers need to be God-centred, giving him the glory for who he is and what he has done. If the creed does not form part of the church's worship, then ensure that at least one prayer is credal in nature, so that God is specifically praised for the life, death and resurrection of his Son.

(3) *God's people need to be given opportunity to confess their sin.* Indeed, worship should naturally lead into confession. For as we see God as he really is, we see ourselves as we really are. Repentance is in fact part of worship, for in repenting we are turning away from 'false idols' and making Jesus Lord of our lives.

(4) *The Scriptures must be brought back into worship.* Leaders need to take seriously the command of Paul to

Timothy: 'Devote yourself to the public reading of Scripture' (1 Tim 4:13). Let there be no half-measures: let God's voice be heard from both Old and New Testaments. Indeed, allow the one to interpret the other. The dictum of John Wesley should be remembered: 'Although there may be chaff in the pulpit, there is always good grain at the lectern'!

(5) *Prayers of intercession should be truly wide-ranging.* Remember the needs not just of the church, but also of the community, the nation and the world. We need to love the world by praying for it (see Matthew 5:44). In a world that as a result of modern communications has shrunk to being a global village, we need to give heed to the warning of Dietrich Bonhoeffer: 'He who denies his neighbour the service of praying for him denies him the service of a Christian.' Let prayers be made for peace, for justice, for healing, for forgiveness — maybe even for judgement. Let God's people pray, 'Your kingdom come.'

In this way non-liturgical churches will begin to fulfil the aim on the Anglican service of Morning Prayer, as expresed in the *Alternative Service Book*:

> We have come together as the family of God
>   in our Father's presence
> to offer him praise and thanksgiving,
> to hear and receive his holy word,
> to bring before him the needs of the world,
> to ask his forgiveness of our sins,
> and to seek his grace,
> that through his Son Jesus Christ
> we may give ourselves to his service.

More importantly, in this way the individual worship needs of God's people will begin to be met.

2. Teaching

People have 'teaching' needs. They have teaching needs in the sense that they need to be taught. Or to put it in another way, God's flock needs to be fed. The sheep need to be led to green pastures. The task of the leader, the pastor, is to meet these needs.

Feeding the flock

Just as a chief duty of a shepherd is to feed his flock by ensuring that they have pasture, so a chief duty of a pastor is to feed the flock from the word of God. As Paul reminds us, in Ephesians 4:11, a pastor by definition is a teacher. Not surprisingly therefore, an essential qualification for the holder of the office of 'bishop' is an ability to teach (1 Tim 3:2; see also 2 Tim 2:4; 1 Tim 5:17; Tit 1:9). In the words of John Stott, 'We are to make the word so plain that they can feed themselves on it with ease, so rich that they can go on sucking its juices during the week ahead, and so tasty that their appetite is whetted for more.'[7]

But does that in fact happen? In some churches, yes, thank God. There are still many evangelical pastors who see teaching as a priority in their ministry. But this is not the case everywhere. John Perry, Bishop of Southampton, as long ago as 1983 wrote:

> I see overwhelming evidence that many congregations are on minimum rations. We soon feel the effect if we never have had a good meal and exist on snacks. But snacks are the diet of many in the local church. Instead of growing up strong and mature in Christ, far too many Christians are spiritually weak and emaciated. Untaught, they are unsure of their spiritual foundations. It is little wonder that they lack the confidence or even the desire to share their faith with others.[8]

John White makes a similar criticism:

> Jesus weeps over sheep fed on lollipops, while the Word of God, the whole Word of God, is edited and reduced to a few favourite passages — Psalm 23, John 3, 1 Corinthians 13 (sentimentally presented and seldom properly examined or expounded), the Galatian epistle, and the Book of Revelation (with explanatory charts)![9]

What has happened? Pastors have failed to teach 'the whole counsel of God' (Acts 20:27). They have fallen back on the purple passages of Scripture. They have failed to take their teaching ministry seriously. 'Tragic to relate,' wrote John Stott, 'many are essentially administrators, whose symbols of ministry are the office rather than the study, and the telephone rather than the Bible.'[10] Of course, administration has a place. Pity the poor leader who fails to take administration seriously! But woe betide the leaders who allow tasks of administration to override their prime task of teaching. Spiritual leadership then crumbles.

Making priorities

The solution to the problem is twofold.

(1) First of all, study needs to become a priority for pastors. Study is the pastor's privilege. According to Luke, the seven 'deacons' were appointed to care for the widows in order to enable the Apostles to give their attention to 'prayer and the ministry of the word' (Acts 6:4). Similarly, pastors today are set aside to give their attention (RSV: 'devote themselves'!) to prayer and the ministry of the word. Pastors therefore need to make the study of God's word their priority. They need to set aside time to read and to dig deep. One would hope that their college course was but an introduction to a lifetime of study. Thus Michael Ramsey, while Archbishop of Canterbury, gave an ordination charge entitled 'Why the Priest?' 'First,' he said, 'the priest is the teacher and preacher, and as such he is *the man of theology*. He is pledged to be a dedicated student of theology; and his study need not be vast in extent, but it will be deep in its integrity, not in order that it may be erudite, but in order that it may be simple. It is those whose studies are shallow who are confused and confusing.'[11]

In even more stark a fashion, John Wesley enunciated similar advice: he told the younger ministers of the Wesleyan societies either to read or to get out of the ministry.[12] Maybe we may infer from 2 Timothy 4:13 that the Apostle Paul himself took study seriously, for he told Timothy: 'When you come, bring ... my scrolls, especially the parchments.'

(2) Preparation needs to become a priority for pastors. It has been said that the churches that are growing today are in the vast majority of cases the churches where preaching and teaching are taken seriously. Now, if preaching and teaching are taken seriously, then this means that sermon preparation becomes an important part of a pastor's ministry. It is not something to be left to Saturdays. It was said of Sir Winston Churchill that, however tired or overworked he was, he never skimped the preparation of one of his speeches. He felt that it should be made with reverential care. The preparation was a tremendous affair to which he gave utmost attention. Surely pastors have an even greater responsibility.

Yes, sermon preparation involves hard work. But hard work in the Lord's service is always rewarded. As James Black once wrote: 'A big ministry is more often the fruit of hard work than the fruit of genius.'[13] Hard work, it is, that meets the needs of the members.

Donald Coggan has a delightful way of describing the preaching task. He refers to it as:

> the joyful tyranny of being a minister of the word ... I use the phrase 'joyful tyranny' advisedly. Preaching *is* a tyranny. I refer not only to the fact that Sunday comes round with an inexorable regularity and makes demands which must needs be met. I refer also to the fact that we know that we must not offer to the Lord a second-rate offering; only the best we can produce will do. I think of the demands which this makes on a man's freshness and devotion and reading and thinking and praying. A tyranny indeed. But a *joyful* tyranny — who would be without it who has been called and commissioned? I suppose a mother finds the care of her family in the early years demanding and tyrannical. But deprive her of her brood and you have the epitome of bereavement and misery.[14]

Furthering maturity

God's people need to be taught. But for what purpose? Surely the aim of Christian teaching is not the imparting of information *per se*, but rather of furthering Christian maturity? Teaching is not an academic exercise, but rather a means to personal development. It is part of the discipleship process.

Such teaching will need to be multi-faceted. It will involve the teaching of the basic doctrines of the faith. It will also involve teaching how to live out the Christian faith. Pastors must not forget that the 'how' is as important as the 'what'. The Canadian pastor, Robert Brow, has made this a particular emphasis:

> Instead of propositional truth, I try to teach beginners *how* to talk to God, how to tell him their doubts and problems, how to thank him. I want to teach them how to forgive and accept forgiveness, how to love their enemies, and how to love their wives or husbands, children or parents. I try to be practical about how each should serve, submit to others, develop personal gifts or talents, cope with strong emotions, use money, and find the way around the Bible for a balanced diet. Doctrine, in the sense of abstract theological statement, comes later.[15]

A balanced diet

This naturally leads me on to talk about the need for pastors to ensure that their people are given a balanced diet. As in the physical realm, so in the spiritual realm, people grow and develop best when they are fed on a balanced diet. Furthermore, a balanced diet doesn't just happen: it is the product of careful planning. The preaching and teaching ministry of the church likewise needs careful planning.

The traditional nonconformist approach to preaching has been to 'leave it to the Spirit'. This was certainly Spurgeon's method. He told his students:

> What is the right text? How do you know it? ... When a verse gives your mind a hearty grip, from which you cannot release yourself. ... Wait for that elect word, even if you wait till within an hour of the service. ... Wait upon the Lord, hear what he would speak, receive the word direct from God's

mouth, and then go forth as an ambassador fresh from the court of heaven.

No doubt some would then argue that if that was good enough for Spurgeon, then it should certainly be good enough for us. Or is it? Is it really the most effective way of bringing God's word to his people? To my mind it is exceedingly wasteful of time, and can also be exceedingly subjective in method. We sense something of the difficulty from Spurgeon himself:

> I confess that I frequently sit hour after hour praying and waiting for a subject, and that this is the main part of my study; much hard labour have I spent in manipulating topics, ruminating upon points of doctrine, making skeletons out of verses, and then burying every bone of them in the catacombs of oblivion!

There is surely a more effective and equally 'spiritual' way of achieving a balanced diet, and that is found in the following of a preaching plan. Thus traditionally the liturgical churches have followed a lectionary. This certainly ensures a balanced diet, for within any given year the lectionary touches on all the main themes of Scripture. Alternatively one can devise one's own preaching plan. This requires a little more effort, but, especially if it involves (short) series of sermons on individual books of the Bible, it can give the congregation the added satisfaction of feeling that they are actually getting to grips with the word of God.

Care, however, is needed to ensure balance. My own rule of thumb in the pastorate was, with the exception of major Christian festivals, on Sunday mornings to preach from the Old Testament in the autumn, from the Gospels in the spring, and from Acts to Revelation in the summer. Needless to say, this also entailed careful planning as far as the rest of the church's teaching programme was concerned — Sunday evenings and the mid-week home groups all had to contribute to the balanced diet. However, with the Spirit's guidance and help it was possible to ensure that the teaching needs of individual members were met.

3. Pastoral care

People have pastoral needs. They have pastoral needs in the sense that they need to experience pastoral care — not just for the acute crisis moments of life, but also for the more ordinary times. Pastoral care needs to be seen as not just helping the hurting, but also encouraging people to grow and develop in the Christian faith. Martin Thornton expresses this thought well when he writes:

> It is curious that what we ambiguously call pastoral care is seen as something entirely negative. It invariably suggests the dispensation of human benevolence with a sprinkling of Christian saccharin: helping those in trouble, counselling the disturbed, solving human problems. This is the ambulance syndrome, implying that Christianity might alleviate suffering but that it has nothing more positive to offer. The pastor is there to pick up the pieces after an accident, and barring accidents he is out of a job.[16]

Wise leaders will seek to meet the pastoral needs of God's people. Indeed, they will want to meet these pastoral needs. Their hearts will warm to the challenge of pastoral care. They scarcely need to be reminded that as shepherds they are called to care for the flock. They will willingly heed the words of the Apostle Peter: 'Be shepherds of God's flock that is under your care, serving as overseers' (1 Pet 5:2).

Caring is demanding

The willingness of the average pastor to engage in pastoral care does not mean that caring for others is an easy business. The very reverse is true. It is a demanding business.

Pastoral care is demanding because the needs are so very diverse. Ezekiel's job description of the Good Shepherd is pertinent here: 'I will seek the lost, and I will bring back the strayed, and I will bind up the crippled, and I will strengthen the weak, and the fat and the strong I will watch over' (Ezek 34:16, RSV). A variety of demands are made on a pastor. Within any given week a pastor could be helping a schizophrenic, comforting a dying patient and his family, counselling a couple whose marriage is on the rocks, confronting a member whose business practices are shady, listening to someone experiencing the pain of redundancy, answering the doubts of a waverer. All this on top of the normal round of pastoral visiting!

Pastoral care is demanding, too, because people are at differing stages of spiritual development. This is beautifully illustrated by William Temple in his commentary on John 21:

> The Lord's questions follow a declining scale: 'Lovest thou me more than these? — Lovest thou me? — Art thou my friend?' But the commissions follow an ascending scale: 'Feed my lambs — tend my sheep — feed my sheep'. The change of expression shows that some change of meaning is intended. 'Feed my lambs': the first charge is to supply the needs of the young of the flock — a task of infinite responsibility, but not as spiritual work is reckoned conspicuously difficult, for the lambs are ready to accept the sustenance offered to them. 'Tend my sheep': the second charge is to exercise general guidance of the flock, including its mature members, a task for one of greater experience than the first. 'Feed my sheep': the third charge is the hardest — to supply the needs of the mature members of the flock; for it is less easy to discern their needs than those of the lambs, and they often have no knowledge of what their own needs are, or, still worse, suppose that they know when in fact they do not.[17]

Whether or not Temple's exegesis of John 21 is correct is a moot point. However, it is true that people are at differing stages of development: there are those who can only take milk, whereas others want to get their teeth into some solid meat! Pastors are thus having constantly to shift gear as they seek to meet people at their different levels.

Thirdly, pastoral care is demanding because people can be so demanding. Not all pastoral situations are 'one-offs'. There are many situations where ongoing support is needed. There are situations where ongoing support is not needed, but nonetheless demanded. There are those who want to use the pastor as a crutch on which to lean, and that constantly. The larger a church becomes the more of a problem these demanding people become. For, if action is not taken, they will either totally drain the pastor, or they will stunt the church's growth. Indeed, the former will also result in the latter. Action therefore has to be taken.

Caring for different types

Gordon MacDonald has helpfully analysed the extent of the pastoral challenge facing a pastor by distinguishing between the VIPs, the VTPs, the VNPs and the VDPs. He writes:

VIPs (the very important people) are 'those you are developing for leadership roles. You share with them your vision for ministry. They are spiritual heavyweights that are really coming along'.

VTPs (the very teachable people) are 'the younger believers who are open to learning and will be tomorrow's leaders'.

VNPs (the very nice people) are 'wonderful to be around, but they make no difference whatsoever as far as the spiritual life of the church is concerned. The church is full of VNPs'.

VDPs (the very draining people) 'the ones who create a negative balance in the arrangement. You're always giving to them, whether it's advice or encouragement or problem solving. You get absolutely no return from them'.

MacDonald adds:

> The VIPs are doing the work now, the VTPs will do the work tomorrow, the VNPs are likely to avoid work whenever possible,

and the VDPs are often the work itself. Most pastors spend their time with groups three and four. We minimize our time with the VIPs because they can take care of themselves. We don't give enough time to the VTPs because the draining people are making such extreme demands on our time. Jesus, however, spent most of his time with the first two groups, and he got them to help with the work of dealing with the other two groups.[18]

In this latter respect Rowley Croucher, in an unpublished paper, made the interesting comment: 'Pastors have often got bogged down in hours of counselling often without any significant results other than the counsellee's knowing they're being supported. But almost any other caring friend could do this just as well.' Pastors need to look after their time. They need to be concerned for priorities.

Sharing responsibilities

Pastors can only cope with all the pastoral needs present in a church as they begin to share the responsibility of pastoral care with others. To a much larger extent than is often appreciated, pastoral care can be delegated.

I have already written of the way in which deacons can share in pastoral care. Indeed, according to Paul Fiddes, 'It is a contradiction in terms to speak of a deacon who is not a pastoral deacon'.[19] Certainly if Acts 6 is a guide, then deacons free their pastor for ministry precisely by being responsible for pastoral care within the church.

However, others too may share in pastoral care. For pastoral care is not the preserve of the pastor. Thus Paul uses the metaphor of the body to bring out the fact that 'the members ... have the ... same care for one another' (1 Cor 12:25, RSV). Similarly, James defines visiting 'orphans and widows in their distress' as the duty of all those whose religion is 'pure and faultless' (Jas 1:27). I have already written of the way in which a 'pastoral team' can have pastoral oversight of the church. Activity leaders — whether Sunday school teachers, youth fellowship leaders, or leaders of the womens' meeting — will inevitably exercise pastoral care over those in their charge. Likewise leaders of house fellowship groups have a clear mandate for pastoral care. In other words, within most churches there are likely to be a variety of systems of pastoral care.

Whatever those systems are, the important thing is that pastoral care is shared. True, the pastor may have the ultimate oversight, but pastors neither can nor should try to be in a close pastoral relationship with all. Their task is to see that all the members of the church are 'covered'.

Establishing priorities

Within the context of shared pastoral care, the pastor can establish priorities for pastoral care.

(1) In the first instance, pastors are called to exercise pastoral care for their families, for their spouses and children. John Perry tells of how, in the opening chapter of his autobiography *Testament of Faith*, William Barclay pays a glowing tribute to his wife, Kate, for the constant support and encouragement she had given him over forty years of marriage:

> There is, though, a touch of sadness, which many a Christian leader — not only clergy — will echo: 'As I come near to the end of my days, the one thing that haunts me more than anything else is that I've been so unsatisfactory a husband and a father. As the Song of Solomon has it: "They made me a keeper of the vineyards; but my own vineyard I have not kept."' When the Pastoral Epistles are laying down the qualifications for the elder, the deacon and the bishop, one of the unvarying demands is that he 'must know how to manage his own household' — and for the minister that is the hardest thing in the world (see Song of Sol 1:6; 1 Tim 3, 4, 12).[20]

If the family is to become a priority, then this means that pastors must make time for them. Indeed, not just any old time, but quality time. Alas, pastors and their families can pass like ships in the night — for night after night pastors are out seeing to the needs of the church. The consequence is that there are many spiritual cripples living in manses: wives who have become bitter against the ministry and the church which their husbands serve; wives who see the church simply as their rival against which they can do so very little. And what is true for some wives can alas be true of some pastors' children too. All the more need for pastors to make a pastoral priority of their families.

(2) Secondly, pastors have a prime responsibility to support their leaders. We have already written of the need of pastors to support their deacons. What is true of their deacons should also be true of the church's activity leaders. Rather than seeking to visit every Tom, Dick and Harry, it is here that pastors should begin.

Howard Snyder makes a similar point when he writes:

> Essentially, the pastor's first priority is to invest himself or herself in a few other persons that they also become disciplers and ministers of Jesus Christ. In fact, no one can effectively pastor more than about a dozen people, if pastoring means discipling. Jesus didn't. This very dilemma, however, may be an opportunity and an invitation to God's design. Today's pastor still cannot improve on what Jesus did. Modern pastors should follow his example. The greatest single contribution a pastor can make to a congregation is to develop a small group of disciples who become ministers and disciples themselves.[21]

Whether or not a pastor limits himself to just twelve people may be a moot point. But the principle is clear: pastors have a prime responsibility for their leaders. Or to express it in Gordon MacDonald's terms, the VIPs and the VTPs should be a pastor's chief concern.

(3) Thirdly, pastors are responsible for the general oversight of the church: their responsibility is to see that everybody is 'covered'. This does not mean that they therefore have to try and constantly visit everybody. The days when a pastor sought to visit everybody on the membership roll at

least once a year are over. On the other hand, this does not mean that pastors will not engage in any general visiting. It is wise and helpful for pastors to seek to ensure that they visit everybody in their care at least once. No hard-and-fast rules can be laid down as to precisely what is involved in general oversight. I would like to feel that, their families and their leaders apart, pastors would major on

— crisis counselling: birth, death, marriage, etc
— the hospitalised
— 'new' people who have just begun to attend church
— those requesting baptism and/or church membership
— general counselling, where requested
— a certain amount of general visiting.

Needless to say, in all these areas pastoral care can and should be shared. Only in this way will all the needs be met.

4. Fellowship

People also have fellowship needs. They have fellowship needs in the sense that they need to experience fellowship. As the Lord God said in the Garden: 'It is not good for the man to be alone. I will make a helper suitable for him' (Gen 2:18). In the original context the reference is to marriage. But what is true of the marriage relationship is true generally. Fellowship is of the essence of being human. Bruce Milne writes: '"What is life if you have not life together?" TS Elliott's question focuses in a poignant manner the agony and the longing of man in our time. For 'life together' is precisely what man reaches out for in his rapidly shrinking planet, and yet what consistently eludes his grasp.'[22]

We need one another. This is the way God has made us. Thus according to the sociologist, George Homans: 'If there is one truth that modern psychology has established it is that an isolated individual is sick. He is sick in mind: he will exhibit disorders of behaviour, emotion and thought.'[23]

Likewise fellowship is of the essence of being Christian. A

solitary Christian is a contradiction in terms. We need to experience 'togetherness'.

But how can the pastoral leader meet this need for fellowship? Not by the encouragement of more and more meetings in the church. Meetings do not necessarily guarantee meeting; meetings do not necessarily guarantee meaningful fellowship. Fellowship is best engendered by the creation and maintenance of small groups. There fellowship in depth can be experienced.

Operating at different levels

The importance of small groups is indicated by the 'five levels of conversation' listed by the Roman Catholic John Powell:

Level 5: *Clichés* — 'Terrible weather we're having these days.'

Level 4: *Re Facts About Others* — 'Did you hear about Mrs So-and-So?'

Level 3: *My Ideas and Judgements* — 'Workers these days are only out for what they can get!'

Level 2: *My Feelings* — 'I'm so relieved! I never realised you felt that way about it.'

Level 1: *Peak Communication (Absolute openness/honesty)* — 'Our relationship hasn't been easy, but I want to tell you that I really value you as my friend.'[24]

People can operate at levels 5, 4 and 3 without much difficulty. Indeed, in a church without small groups, the level of conversation is almost without exception conducted within those three levels. Where, however, the church is broken down into small groups, there conversation at level 2 is possible. If the small group is really open, level 1 may occasionally be touched too.

Creating fellowship groups

Fellowship in depth is best encouraged through the creation and maintenance of small groups. This is no modern discovery. Listen to George Whitfield:

My brethren, let us plainly and freely tell one another what God has done for our souls. To this end you would do well, as others have done, to form yourselves into little companies of four or five each, and meet once a week to tell each other what is in your hearts: that you may then pray for and comfort each other as need shall require. None but those who have experienced it can tell the unspeakable advantages of such a union and communion of souls. ... None I think that truly loves his own soul and his brethren as himself, will be shy of opening his heart, in order to have their advice, reproof, admonition and prayers, as occasion requires. A sincere person will esteem it one of the greatest blessings.

Small groups are essential for the following reasons.

(i)   Love can be expressed there.   People today are crying out to be affirmed, to be valued. But how can anyone be loved, affirmed or valued within a crowd? Fellowship groups are the answer, for there relationships can develop, strong bonds of friendship can be formed, and people begin to feel wanted and loved — warts and all! Only in this way can many begin to fulfil the command of Jesus to 'truly love one another as I have loved you' (Jn 13:34–35).

(ii)   Life can be shared there.   In the thinking reflected in the New Testament, 'fellowship' involved more than simply being good friends. Fellowship involved caring for one another, carrying each other's burdens, encouraging one another and building one another up, and praying for one another (see 1 Cor 12:25; Gal 6:2; 1 Thess 5:11; Jas 5:16). Such 'one anotherness' can only take place within the context of the small group.

(iii)   Maturity can be developed there.   If people are to develop in the Christian life, then they need both encouragement and correction – and this is possible within the context of a fellowship group. Ephesians 4:15–16 is a beautiful

picture of the way in which Christians can minister by 'speaking the truth in love' to one another and in this way helping one another to mature in the faith.

(iv) Gifts can be discovered there. Spiritual gifts are often best discovered through the process of 'trial and error'. However, if people are to be encouraged to experiment as they seek to discover and use their gifts, then almost certainly they will need the intimacy and security of the small group. For it is only when people are among friends that it doesn't seem to matter if they fall flat on their face — they know that the others in the group will love them, whatever. Paul's word to the Romans is pertinent: 'Having gifts that differ according to the grace given to us, let us use them: if prophecy, in proportion to our faith' (Rom 12:6). Whatever the gift, 'faith' is normally best sparked off within the security of the fellowship group.

Covenanting together

It must be confessed that there is no magic in the small group. The mere fact that a group meets within a home every other week is no guarantee that they will truly function as living cells of the body. People can meet together until the cows go home, but they may never truly build one another up in love. Small groups can only begin to be successful when there is a joint willingness to be open and honest.

Such openness is not easy. For if people are to be open to one another, then they must throw their masks away — and throwing masks away is dangerous, because people will then see them as they really are. This then proves not a little embarrassing (indeed, is not nakedness of any variety embarrassing?) because the truth is then revealed. People are then seen not to be as 'lovable' or as 'spiritual' as they would have others see them.

John Powell once expressed the fears that people have in being open with one another in these words: 'I am afraid to tell you who I am, because, if I tell you who I am, you may not like who I am, and it's all that I have.'[25] However, Christ calls us to be true to ourselves: for it is only so that we can receive help and ministry from others. It is only so that we can experience true fellowship.

Dietrich Bonhoeffer once put it this way:

> Just as surely as God desires to lead us to a knowledge of genuine Christian fellowship, so surely must we be overwhelmed by a great disillusionment with others, with Christians in general, and, if we are fortunate, with ourselves. ... God is not a God of the emotion, but the God of truth. Only that fellowship which faces such disillusionment, with all its unhappy and ugly aspects, begins to be what it is and should be in God's sight. ... When the morning mists of dreams vanish, then dawns the bright day of Christian fellowship.[26]

There is a cost involved in genuine fellowship. A cost reflected in a commitment to be oneself, and a commitment to love the others in the group, whatever is revealed.

One sure way to ensure that a fellowship group lives up to its name is to encourage the group to form a 'covenant' together. A biblical parallel to this practice may perhaps be found in the story of David and Jonathan, who made a covenant together (1 Sam 18:3–4). In this instance, when Saul came out to seek David's life and David was afraid, Jonathan went to David and 'helped him to find strength in God' (1 Sam 23:15–16), or as the RSV renders it: Jonathan 'strengthened his hand in God'. Likewise present-day 'covenant' groups seek to strengthen one another in God, for this is what true fellowship is all about. In the words of Thomas à Kempis:

> Were all men saints, what would be left for us to bear
> At others' hands to please our God?
> But now has God ordained
> That we should learn to carry each the burden of another.
> None is without his failings, none without his burden,
> None strong enough for his own needs, none wise enough.

We take our turns to lift the burden from each other.
We take our turns to comfort and console,
To help, counsel and teach.[27]

As I have already indicated, fellowship involves far more than the mutual strengthening of one another in moments of weakness. It also involves mutual accountability with a view to encouraging growth in the Christian life. It was this kind of in-depth fellowship which members of the early Methodist class system experienced. For each time they met, the following four questions had to be asked of one another: What known sins have you committed since our last meeting? What temptations have you met with? How were you delivered? What have you thought, said or done of which you doubt whether it be a sin or not? We need to continue to ask these kinds of questions of one another. For only where we are ruthlessly honest with one another is there any hope of people being helped forwards in the Christian life. Clearly such intimate questions cannot be asked with ease in every group. They can, however, be asked within the context of a 'covenant' group, where members are committed to one another. Thus covenant groups have been likened to 'weight-watchers' meetings where individuals commit themselves to a programme of change and use the rest of the group for support and encouragement in their task.

Drawing up a covenant

To create such a covenant, a fellowship group needs to agree on a number of covenant 'disciplines' to which the members of the group commit themselves to adhere. Ideally each group should write its own covenant. A specimen covenant, however, is provided by Lyman Coleman:

For the duration of this series we agree to the following disciplines as a group:

Attendance: To give priority to the group meetings. Except for emergencies we will be present and on time.

Participation: To give ourselves to the purpose of the group and become a spiritual community — by sharing our 'stories' with one another.

Confidentiality: To keep anything that is shared strictly confidential.

Accountability: To allow the rest of the group to hold each of us accountable to the goals we set for ourselves.

Support: To give each other the right to call on one another for help and support in times of temptation and need — even in the middle of the night. We realise that we need the help of each other to overcome temptation, spiritual depression, and weakness.

Evangelism: To be willing and ready at any time to welcome newcomers into the group who need its support and help, and who will agree to these minimum disciplines.[28]

I find this a challenging and helpful covenant. Note, in particular, the second discipline: participation. This is basically the discipline of 'openness'. It is only as people open themselves up to one another that real progress can be made in the Christian life. Then we discover we are not the only spiritual 'pygmies'. Few, if any, are living the ideal (normal?) Christian life. It is when we are honest with ourselves and with one another that we can begin to receive ministry and help.

My one quibble with this example of a group covenant is that I do not believe that such fellowship groups can normally be evangelistic in nature. Hence my difficulty with the last discipline. Yes, it is good for any group to be open to newcomers (who 'will agree to these minimum disciplines'). However, for true fellowship to take place there must surely be as a prerequisite an initial commitment to Jesus Christ.

5. Service

People have service needs. They have a need to exercise meaningful service for their Lord. They desire to respond to God's grace, but all too often do not know how to do so.

One of the tasks of the leader is to make such service possible. In the words of Paul, the pastor-teacher is 'to prepare God's people for works of service' (Eph 4:12), or as the RSV translates: 'to equip the saints for the work of ministry'.

Yes, far from monopolising ministry, the pastor is called to multiply ministry. If, as Morton Gibbs suggested, God's people have been 'frozen', then the pastor's task is to defrost them and mobilise them for service! God has given gifts to his church. The pastor's task is to encourage the use of these gifts, both within and outside the church. Thus Douglas Webster defines the pastoral task in these terms:

> The special responsibility of the clergy is to enable every Christian for whom they have pastoral care to find some form of active ministry, however humble, to see their daily work in terms of ministry and witness, and by encouragement to keep them up to the mark.[29]

An alternative definition of the task is given by the Swiss theologian, Hans Ruedi Weber: 'The laity are not helpers of the clergy, so that the clergy can do their job, but the clergy are helpers of the whole people of God, so that they can do their job.'[30]

Enabling ministry

A variety of metaphors have been drawn on to describe the pastor's role in encouraging and enabling the individual members of the church to get on with their ministry. As we shall see, some are more helpful than others. Yet each encourages a facet of this often neglected, albeit vital, part of a pastor's ministry.

The conductor. Michael Griffiths likened the pastor to a conductor: 'In an orchestra the task of the conductor is to get all the members functioning together and playing in harmony. It is not his job to dash around the seats playing all the instruments himself one after another.'[31] How true! No pastor has a monopoly on the Spirit's gifts.

The coach. Others have likened the pastor to the coach standing on the sidelines, encouraging and helping the players. On this model the pastor, like the coach, is not really an active member of the team. Alan Stibbs has somewhere likened the pastor to a rowing coach: 'His distinctive task is to get every member pulling his weight, and to train them as a crew to row effectively together.' One disadvantage of this rowing imagery is that the team then appear rather monochrome: they are all performing the same task — rowing!

The rugby captain. Tom Cadman of New Zealand argues that the pastor is more actively involved in the team than has sometimes been suggested:

> In New Zealand we have two favourite sports, cricket in the summer and rugby football in the winter. In cricket, one man can virtually win the day. If he scores many runs when batting and bowls out several of the opposition when fielding, it is possible for other team members to fail or stand around him and watch him produce results. With rugby this seldom if ever happens. For the whole game, the whole team is on the field, including the captain. He must lead and inspire but without a team effort, it is virtually impossible for one man to win the game. The image Paul uses of the ministry is akin to that of a rugby captain rather than that of a cricket captain. Ministers are encouragers of the team, all of whom are engaged in mission. At no point of the game can they be spectators. Sadly the pattern we have developed is that of the minister as 'super-player', who, by his skill and prowess, keeps the team going whilst most of the players spend their time in the pavilion (pews) hoping he will not let them down![32]

I believe that there is much to be commended in this particular metaphor.

The mayonnaise(!).   This unusual and amusing metaphor has been developed by Andrew Le Peau: 'Perhaps you've heard the commercial for Hellmann's mayonnaise. "Bring out the Hellmann's ... bring out the best!" The pun is apt. ... Facilitators are people who bring out the best in others. They are able to draw out the strengths in people without drawing attention to themselves. Like mayonnaise, they may not be noticed. But without facilitators, it is not as good.'[33] Pastors bring out the best in other people. That is a helpful emphasis. It is reminiscent of Lao-tse's definition of leadership: 'A leader is best when people barely know he exists.'

The petrol-pump attendant.   Michael Green has likened the pastor to the petrol-pump attendant whose task it is 'to get others mobile'.[34] I don't find this a very attractive metaphor! It makes pastoral ministry sound far more mechanical than in fact it is.

Clearly, all the above metaphors have their strengths and weaknesses. Their strengths ultimately outweigh their weaknesses in that all of them, in one way or the other, draw attention to the key role which the pastor has in encouraging and enabling others to serve. This role cannot be overemphasised.

Releasing the gifts

How do pastors 'prepare God's people for works of service'? How do they release the gifts present in the body of Christ? How do they enable individuals to engage in meaningful service?

A number of ways might be suggested in which the members of a local church might be encouraged to discover and use their gifts in Christian service:

(i) By teaching.   Constant teaching on the importance and usefulness of every limb in the body is essential. In the words of James Kennedy, so many Christians still believe

that 'clerical George' should do it all.[35] People need to be taught that every-member ministry is a scriptural norm.

(ii) By modelling. It is no good if the pastor preaches every-member ministry, but in actual fact persists in doing everything of significance in the church. Pastors must practise what they preach and encourage their people to be engaged in pastoral care, teaching, evangelism and social service and action of every kind.

(iii) By identifying gifts. One of the tasks of a pastor is to spot potential within people. Just as Jesus spotted the possibilities within Peter (see John 1:42), so too should a pastor be quick to spot, and then encourage, gifts within others.

(iv) By training. Gifts need to be developed through training. One who has made 'lay'-training a speciality is Clarry Hendrickse. In *One Urban Church and Lay Ministry* he writes:

> There need to be constant growth opportunities to enable a person's growth in Christ to be sustained ... I have found it helpful in the summer of each year to think prayerfully about each church member and which new teaching opportunity for service ought to be offered to him in the autumn round of courses. I then write to each person inviting him to take this next step.[36]

In his book Hendrickse described how he ran a basic training course of eight sessions where people were given an opportunity to discover what their gifts were. He then drew up an individual contract of a year, with a mandatory review after three months. This contract included the individual's prayer discipline, leading in public worship, personal family responsibilities, areas of work related to personal gifts, suggestions for further study and conferences! Hendrickse presents a challenge to the rest of the church to take training seriously. It may be objected that what he outlined is only possible within the context of a small church. But is it? Pastors of large churches could consider drawing up individual contracts, in the first place at least, for their leaders. That at least would be a beginning!

(v) By exposure.   People frequently have no idea of their gifts until they are exposed to some situation and then encouraged to launch out. Douglas Webster, with the missionary situation in view, talks of the unwillingness people sometimes have to trust those they have trained. 'Jesus had no protective attitude to his trainees; he let them make mistakes, he left them long before they fully understood the Gospel they were to proclaim. . . Instead he promised them the Holy Spirit who would teach them everything and guide them into all truth (John 14:23; 16:13).'[37] Webster then goes on to ask whether one reason for the rapid growth of the Pentecostal churches in Latin America could be 'their reliance on the Spirit rather than on a theological syllabus and academic qualifications'. Pastors need to be risk-takers — this seems to be the clear lesson Webster is saying!

(vi) By means of house groups.   House groups have been described as 'leader-breeders'. We have already referred to the way in which in the intimacy of the fellowship group people will venture into an area of ministry which they would never attempt in public. Michael Green suggests that at least once a year it would be good to have an evening when members share what they would really love to do in Christ's service: 'Our own spiritual desires are often an indication of potential gifts.' He goes on, 'Another evening could be given over to affirming one another: "What I most appreciate about you is . . . ." ' Often people are astonished to discover gifts in this way. And gifts discovered and tested in the small group may subsequently become important in the church at large'.[38]

(vii) By involvement. Once people's gifts have been recognised and they have received training in the use of them, then they should be given a sphere in which to exercise them. Gifts need to be released for service. An obvious point, but a necessary one.

Ensuring priority

Equipping and enabling people to serve is no optional extra to pastoral ministry. It lies at the heart. 'By all means' pastors should seek to equip and enable their people to serve.

The priority of enabling all God's people to fulfil their ministry is firmly expressed by John Tiller: 'The full-time priest should be seen as a support for the local church with its indigenous ministry.' Instead of an incumbent providing a GP service, Tiller envisaged a lay eldership running the church, with the stipendiary priest outside as 'a provider of external resources and vision for the local church's ministry'.[39] Although I peronally see the normal role of the pastor as within — and not without — the local church, I welcome the emphasis that John Tiller makes. John Tiller is not being radical in likening the pastor to a resource person, he is simply being scriptural. Ministry does not begin and end with the pastor. In other words, the ministry of the whole people of God is not an addendum to the ministry of the church. It is the normal ministry of the church. All the more reason therefore to do away with using the term 'ministry' for the ministry of the church's 'professionals'! Ministry belongs to all God's people. The task of the pastor is to make that ministry possible.

Notes

1. David Owen, *Sharers in Worship* (National Christian Education Council: Redhill, 1980), p 23.
2. William Temple, *Readings in St John's Gospel* (Macmillan: London, 1961), p 68.

3. David Owen, *op cit*, p 24.
4. Ralph Martin, *The Worship of God* (Eerdmans: Grand Rapids, MI, 1982), p 4.
5. Donald English, *God in the Gallery* (Epworth: London, 1975), p 11.
6. Ralph Martin, *op cit*, p 5.
7. John Stott, *The Call to Preach* (London Baptist Preachers Association Diamond Jubilee lecture 1968).
8. John Perry, *Christian Leadership* (Hodder and Stoughton: London, 1983), p 17.
9. John White, *Flirting with the World* (Hodder and Stoughton: London, 1983), p 128.
10. John Stott, *I Believe in Preaching* (Hodder and Stoughton: London, 1982), p 124.
11. Michael Ramsey, *The Christian Priest Today* (SPCK: London, 1985), p 7.
12. Quoted by Oswald Chambers, *Spiritual Leadership* (Marshalls: London, 1967), p 95.
13. James Black, *The Mystery of Preaching* (Marshall, Morgan and Scott: London, 1977), p 41.
14. Donald Coggan, *On Preaching* (SPCK: London, 1978), pp 3–4.
15. Robert Brow, *Go Make Learners* (Harold Shaw: Wheaton, I1, 1981), p 24.
16. Martin Thornton, *Spiritual Direction* (SPCK: London, 1984), pp 9–10.
17. William Temple, *op cit*, p 386.
18. Gordon MacDonald, article in *Leadership*, vol 5, no 4, p 111.
19. Paul Fiddes, *A Leading Question* (Baptist Union: London), p 38.
20. John Perry, *op cit*, p 20.
21. Howard Snyder, *Liberating the Church* (Marshalls: Basingstoke, 1983), p 248 f.
22. Bruce Milne, *We Belong Together* (InterVarsity Press: Leicester, 1978), p 9.
23. Quoted by Michael Harper, *You Are My Sons* (Hodder and Stoughton: London, 1979), p 120.
24. John Powell, *Why Am I Afraid To Tell You Who I Am?* (Fontana: London, 1975), pp 50–62.
25. *Ibid*, p 20.

26. Dietrich Bonhoeffer, *Life Together* (SCM: London, 1976), p 15.
27. Thomas à Kempis, *The Imitation of Christ* (I XVI).
28. Lyman Coleman, *Are You Together?* (Scripture Union: London, 1987), p 4.
29. Douglas Webster, *Not Ashamed* (Hodder and Stoughton: London, 1970), p 55.
30. Quoted by Douglas Webster, *op cit*, p 54.
31. Michael Griffiths, *Cinderella with Amnesia* (InterVarsity Press: London, 1975), p 59.
32. Tom Cadman, 'How I Practise My Ministry', *Baptist World Alliance Commission on Pastoral Leadership* (Maclean, VA, 1982).
33. Andrew Le Peau, *Paths of Leadership* (Scripture Union: London, 1984), p 52.
34. Michael Green, *Freed to Serve* (Hodder and Stoughton: London, 1983), p 35.
35. James Kennedy, *Evangelism Explosion* (Coverdale: London, 1982), p 5.
36. Clarry Hendrickse, *One Inner Urban Church and Lay Ministry* (Grove: Bramcote, 1983), pp 10, 12.
37. Douglas Webster, *op cit*, pp 23–24.
38. Michael Green, *op cit*, p 133.
39. John Tiller, *A Strategy for the Church's Ministry* (CIO Publishing: London, 1983), p 117.

9
The Leader: Qualities for Leadership

What kind of a person best works as a senior partner with others to achieve the task, build the team and meet individual needs? What qualities are needed for leadership? It is this question which we now seek to address.

1. Qualities for secular leadership

John Adair has an interesting exercise entitled 'Have you got what it takes for a top job in leadership?' The object of the exercise is to place the following attributes in order of 'most valuable at the top level of management' by placing a number 1 to 25 beside them:

Ambition
Willingness to work hard
Enterprise
Astuteness
Ability to 'stick at it'
Capacity for lucid writing
Imagination
Ability to spot opportunities
Willingness to work long hours
Curiosity

Understanding of others'
Skill with numbers
Capacity for abstract thought
Integrity
Ability to administer efficiently
Enthusiasm
Capacity to speak lucidly
Singlemindedness
Willingness to take risks
Leadership
Ability to take decisions
Analytical ability
Ability to meet unpleasant situations
Open-mindedness
Ability to adapt quickly to change

Having gone through the first stage of the exercise, the second stage is to compare one's answers with the ratings given to these attributed by a cross-section of successful chief executives. Their listing of 'most valuable' qualities makes fascinating reading:

1 Ability to take decisions
2 Leadership
3 Integrity
4 Enthusiasm
5 Imagination
6 Willingness to work hard
7 Analytical ability
8 Understanding of others
9 Ability to spot opportunities
10 Ability to meet unpleasant situations
11 Ability to adapt quickly to change
12 Willingness to take risks
13 Enterprise
14 Capacity to speak lucidly
15 Astuteness
16 Ability to administer efficiently
17 Open-mindedness

18 Ability to 'stick to it'
19 Willingness to work long hours
20 Ambition
21 Single-mindedness
22 Capacity for lucid writing
23 Curiosity
24 Skill with numbers
25 Capacity for abstract thought[1]

I confess I am somewhat relieved that 'skill with numbers' comes so far down on the list of most valuable qualities! There is certainly food for thought in this listing.

2. Qualities for pastoral leadership

But are there particular qualities necessary for pastoral leadership? It is interesting, if not instructive, to review the host of possibilities that have been suggested. We take at random six such lists of necessary qualities for pastoral leadership.

Three 'qualities for success'

Charles Simpson lists character, capacity and charisma as the three indispensable qualities for success in pastoral leadership. He subdivides the second quality into six key capacities:

the capacity to learn
the capacity to communicate
the capacity to maintain the body-life of the church
the capacity for a global perspective
the capacity to handle pressure
the capacity for hard work.[2]

Six qualities needed for a new pastor

According to Peter Wagner, the following six qualities are needed in a pastor who will help the church to grow:
(1) The pastor must be a leader. Look for a person who is called to be out front.

(2) The pastor must be a person of faith. A person of faith is focused on tomorrow rather than yesterday. Setting goals comes naturally to such a leader.

(3) The pastor must be a possibility thinker. Possibility thinkers know how to turn problems into opportunities. Faith sets the direction, possibility thinking discovers creative ways of getting the job done.

(4) The pastor must be a good preacher. Don't confuse communication, which is highly important, with eloquence, which is of minimal importance.

(5) The pastor must be flexible. Church growth means constant change. Ask God for a person who knows when to change in the light of fresh challenges.

(6) The pastor must be a hard worker. 'Most effective pastors share one common characteristic: each is a remarkably hard worker' (Lyle Schaller).[3]

Seven ingredients for a leader

Oswald Sanders believed that Montgomery's seven ingredients necessary in a leader in war are appropriate to the spiritual warfare in which the church is engaged:

(1) He should be able to sit back and avoid getting immersed in detail.

(2) He must not be petty.

(3) He must not be pompous.

(4) He must be a good picker of men.

(5) He should trust those under him, and let them get on with their job without interference.

(6) He must have the power of clear decision.

(7) He should inspire confidence.[4]

Eight personality traits of a leader

Ted Engstrom lists eight traits common to all who are effective spiritual leaders:

(1) enthusiasm

(2) trustworthiness

(3) self-discipline

(4) decisiveness
(5) courage
(6) humour
(7) loyalty
(8) unselfishness

According to Engstrom:

> It is vital that people striving to lead others take the necessary measures to learn the techniques and develop those traits which will enhance their effectiveness. Merely emulating someone else will not bring about the desired ends. ... It can come about only by learning one's weaknesses, evaluating the hindrance to change and then utilizing this knowledge by putting it to work to develop the strengths to the maximum.[5]

Nine tests of leadership

In addition to Montgomery's seven ingredients, Oswald Sanders also quoted approvingly the nine tests of John Mott, one of the early pioneers of the ecumenical movement:

(1) Does he do little things well?
(2) Has he learned the meaning of priorities?
(3) How does he use his leisure?
(4) Has he intensity?
(5) Has he learned to take advantage of momentum?
(6) Has he the power of growth?
(7) What is his attitude to discouragements?
(8) How does he face impossible situations?
(9) What are his weakest points?[6]

Twelve principles of leadership

Finally, in this brief survey let me mention John Haggai's twelve principles. According to Haggai:

> These principles are not skills — although skills may be used to enhance them — but they are characteristics. They are those factors that make a leader different from other people. Developing these principles will help you to fulfil the responsibilities of your leadership position in the most effective way.[7]

It takes little rewriting of the terms to turn these characteristics into qualities.

Haggai's principles are as follows:

(1) vision
(2) goal-setting
(3) love
(4) humility
(5) self-control
(6) communication
(7) investment
(8) opportunity
(9) energy
(10) staying power
(11) authority
(12) awareness

All these lists of qualities make fascinating and indeed helpful reading. At the end of the day one cannot argue that one list is essentially more correct than another. The fact is that every list is a reflection of truth. There is something to be learnt from each one of them.

However, without taking away from any of the qualities listed, I would wish to argue that there are six particular qualities which are vital for effective pastoral leadership. Each of the six is indeed quite indispensable. Pastoral leadership without them is, if not unthinkable, then much the poorer.

3 Six key qualities for pastoral leadership

Vision

First and foremost a leader must be a visionary. Vision is essential to leadership. In the words of Proverbs 29:18 (Authorised Version): 'Where there is no vision, the people perish.' Unfortunately the AV rendering here is almost certainly a mistranslation of the Hebrew (NIV renders this verse: 'Where there is no revelation, the people cast off restraint'). Nonetheless it remains a true statement. For a church to grow and develop it must have a sense of purpose and direction. Such purpose and direction is spearheaded by the leader. It is the leader who knows the task that is to be achieved.

The importance of this key quality is brought out by Ronald Knox in the conclusion of his book *Enthusiasm*:

> Men will not live without vision; that moral we do well to carry away with us from contemplating, is so many strange forms, the record of visionaries. If we are content with the humdrum, the second-best, the hand-over-hand, it will not be forgiven us.[8]

A caretaker may serve a building, but he cannot serve a church. The church is an army on the move, and what an army needs is a leader with a sense of strategy. Vision is of the essence of leadership.

It was Napoleon who once defined a leader as 'a dealer in hope'. This arresting definition can have a twofold application to pastoral leadership. First of all, a pastor is a dealer of hope in terms of 'macrovision'. In a world that is marred on both a personal and corporate level by tragedy and futility, pastors are called to point to the new world that is coming. The pastor is the preacher who announces the good news of the kingdom; who proclaims that one day 'right' and not just 'might' will triumph; who assures God's people that the world is not moving on to chaos — it is moving on to Christ. Such hope, founded on the raising of Jesus from the dead, is to be the content of the church's proclamation Sunday by Sunday. Any celebration of the Lord's Supper worthy of the name is a moment when people are pointed beyond the disappointments and frustrations, if not the sufferings, of the present, to the day when God's people shall eat and drink at the marriage supper of the Lamb. Vision involves eschatology!

But along with this 'macrovision' there is also 'microvision'.

Leaders are called to give people a vision of what God intends for the life of their local church. Pastors are not in the business of maintaining the status quo, but of leading God's people onwards to the new pattern God intends for his children. It is the task of leaders to encourage their churches to be 'sunrise people' dreaming of the future, rather than 'sunset people' dreaming of the past!

Leaders, in the language of Robert Schuller, are called to be 'possibility thinkers', men and women who refuse to limit their God:

> God has unlimited financial resources and unlimited intelligence to achieve his goals. Possibility thinking is simply opening your mind for God to unfold the ways in which His will can be accomplished. Thus God performs miracles in the people who, unafraid of failure and public embarrassment, move boldly and bravely forward attempting big things for God and expecting great things from God.[9]

Leaders are those who are imbued with the spirit enshrined in the words of George Bernard Shaw: 'You see things as they are and ask "why?" But I dream things that never were, and ask "why not?"' Leaders are great optimists, but optimists in the best sense of the word: for suffering neither from false optimism, which ignores or dismisses problems, nor from pessimism, which allows people to be crippled by the problems that are around them, visionary leaders are those who see the problems in the light of God's word that he 'is able to do far more than all we ask or imagine, according to his power that is at work within us' (Eph 3:20). There is spiritual truth in the comment of Henry Kissenger: 'The great man understands the essence of a problem, the ordinary man sees only the symptoms. ... The great man has a vision of the future which enables him to place obstacles into perspective; the ordinary leader turns pebbles in the road into boulders.'[10]

Enthusiasm

Vision in itself is insufficient. Enthusiasm is equally vital. Enthusiasm is needed to communicate the vision to the people, and in turn to excite others with that vision. Enthusiasm it is which enables a leader truly to influence others. Without enthusiasm there is no influence, there is no leadership. Conversely, where there is enthusiasm combined with vision, there is leadership. Thus Charles Schwab, the man to whom Andrew Carnegie paid $1 million a year because of his ability to motivate people, once said, 'A man can succeed at almost anything for which he has unlimited enthusiasm.'[11]

The importance of enthusiasm comes to the fore in Montgomery's definition of leadership. Leadership, Montgomery said, is 'the capacity to rally men and women to a common purpose, and the character which inspires confidence'. A leader 'must exercise an effective influence, and the degree to which he can do this will depend on the personality of the man — the *incandescence* of which he is capable, the flame which burns within him, the magnetism which will draw the hearts of men towards him'. An example of such magnetism was given somewhat graphically by a Southern Baptist pastor, who once declared, 'My church would charge Hell with a thimble-full of water, if I said this was where God wants us to go.'

Enthusiasm has never had the best of presses in Britain. More often than not it has been seen as the trait of a madman rather than a leader. Thus in the nineteenth century Disraeli once counselled Queen Victoria against appointing Bishop Tait as Archbishop of Canterbury, for, he said, 'There is in his idiosyncracy a strange fund of enthusiasm, a quality which ought never to be possessed by an Archbishop of Canterbury or a Prime Minister of England.' Enthusiasm clearly was seen as undignified for one holding a high office. A century or more before, the respected Baptist statesman John Ryland said to William Carey at a ministers' fraternal:

'Sit down, young man, you're an enthusiast! If God wishes to convert the heathen he'll do so without your aid or mine.' Yet in fact it was precisely the enthusiasm of a young man like Carey that God needed to begin the modern missionary movement, which in turn has been responsible for the conversion of many a 'heathen'!

There is nothing wrong with enthusiasm. Indeed, there is everything to be said for it. For although enthusiasm can be a very human quality, it is first and foremost a spiritual one. Indeed, the word literally means 'possession by God'. Rightly understood, enthusiasm is a quality generated by the Holy Spirit. Enthusiasts are men and women fired by God's Spirit. 'Fan into flame the gift of God, which is in you through the laying on of my hands,' said Paul to the young leader, Timothy. 'For God did not give us a spirit of timidity, but a spirit of power, of love and of self-discipline' (2 Tim 1:6–7).

Enthusiasm is therefore to be encouraged. It is faith looking into the future and committing itself in the face of the seemingly impossible. But to the Christian enthusiast the probabilities are always favourable. Convinced that God is with them, enthusiasts have no fear of the present or future, for 'in all these things we are more than conquerors' (see Rom 8:31–39).

Enthusiasm is accordingly a quality to be desired. Morris West in his novel *The Shoes of the Fisherman* has the cardinals ask the newly elected pope, '*Quid vobis videtis*? What do you want?' The pope replied, 'Find me men with fire in their hearts and wings on their feet.' John Perry goes on to make the comment: 'What astute insight! In his search for leaders in his Church, God is always on the look-out for people who have the fire of the Spirit in their hearts and the wings of obedience on their feet.'[12]

To return to our theme, enthusiasm produces greater commitment to the task, creates team spirit, and enthuses the individual. It is indeed a desirable quality.

Industry

A third equally vital quality is that of industry: ie, the willingness to work hard. Vision and enthusiasm get nowhere without the backbreaking work involved in implementing the vision. Thomas Alva Edison was surely right when he defined genius as '1% inspiration and 99% perspiration'. It is not sufficient to have a bright idea: ideas require work to be done on them if they are ever to develop beyond the merely theoretical stage and actually benefit a community. Thus William Morris, who later became Lord Nuffield, and who began his career repairing bicycles and ended up founding a mighty industrial empire, when asked to account for the secret of his success, replied that it was 'creative imagination wedded to indomitable industry'.[13]

In whatever profession, hard work is essential to success. Thus Paderewski, the world-renowned pianist, was once congratulated by Queen Victoria after she had heard him play: 'Mr Paderewski, you are a genius.' 'That may be, Ma'am,' he replied, 'but before I was a genius, I was a drudge.' Success involved literally hours of practice. Indeed, it was not unknown for him to repeat a bar or phrase fifty times to perfect it.[14]

Turning to a totally different sphere of life, Lord Thomson of Fleet, the former newspaper magnate, once said, 'If I have any advice to pass on, it is this: if one wants to be successful, one must think until it hurts. One must worry a problem in one's mind until it seems there cannot be another aspect of it that hasn't been considered. Believe me, that is hard work and, from my close observation, I can say that there are few people indeed who are prepared to perform this arduous and tiring work.'[15]

If hard work is vital in the secular world, it is equally vital in the world of the church. Alas, in this age of 'instant everything', it is sometimes assumed that God will allow us to short-circuit the process. If we have sufficient faith, then God will bring about whatever we seek to achieve. But, although it is God who gives the growth, we have to 'plant' and 'water' (see 1 Corinthians 3:6). The secret of the Apostle Paul's greatness is to be found from one perspective in the grace of God, but from another equally valid perspective it is to be found in the fact that Paul worked harder than all the other Apostles (1 Cor 15:10). Long before Winston Churchill's speech to the House of Commons on 13th May 1940, Paul knew what it was to experience 'blood, toil, tears and sweat' (see 2 Corinthians 11:23–28).

The temptation today is to 'leave it to the Spirit', as if leaving it to the Spirit effectively discharges us from all responsibility. But this is far from the truth. The words of Bob Roxburgh need to be heeded:

> Renewal is not all a matter of being 'blessed'. It is the hard work of implementing dreams through organisation, structures and strategy through the empowering and enabling of the Holy Spirit. . . . Most church success stories have as much perspiration as inspiration behind them in the sense that members have worked hard to establish structures and strategies that will fulfil the prompting and vision of the Spirit.[16]

There is no substitute for hard work!

Rightly or wrongly, no pastor will lead a church to growth or enable it to make a significant impact on the community without being prepared to work hard. Pastors who begin their working-day late, end it early, and litter it with endless cups of coffee or tea will not get very far, however much they may dream dreams and see visions. People of vision need to become people of action and action in turn involves hard work!

Perseverance

Closely allied to industry is perseverance. The leader must be prepared to 'work at it'. In the words of Samuel Johnson: 'Great works are performed not by strength, but by perseverance.' It is the will to persevere that is often the difference between failure and success. The vision may be right, but the vision may not be easily realised.

John Stott tells the story of Thomas Sutcliffe Mort who was determined to solve the problem of refrigeration so that meat could be exported from Australia to Britain. He gave himself three years in which to do it, but in fact it took him twenty-six years. He lived long enough to see the first shipment of refrigerated meat leave Sydney, but died before learning whether it had reached its destination safely. He had, however, lived long enough to realise his family motto: 'To persevere is to succeed' (a play on their Huguenot family name: 'Fidele à la Mort').[17]

Perseverance is necessary in Christian leadership not because of technical difficulties (which principally dogged Thomas Mort), but because of people difficulties. However right the vision, history has frequently proved that the people of God have sometimes been slow to catch the vision, and that process can take time. Perseverance allied to patience is needed.

Perseverance involves long-term commitment to a project. It takes time to begin to work out a vision. In other words, short-term pastorates on the whole will achieve relatively little. Pastoral longevity is called for. As Peter Wagner rightly states:

When you accept a call to an existing church, you are on probation for three to six years. This is what is behind Lyle Schaller's observation that the productive years of a given pastorate begin around years four, five or six. It takes that long to earn your right to lead by proving that you are a servant.[18]

This finding was confirmed in the survey of English Baptist churches that Alan Wilkinson and I undertook: 'It is not until a minister has served for five to ten years in his church that a bias towards growth becomes evident. In other words, it takes time for fruit to emerge from someone's ministry.'[19]

But perseverance involves more than patience. It involves

resilience too. This is why the popular adage of Josh Billings — 'Consider the postage stamp ... its usefulness consists in sticking to one thing till it gets there!' — is not exactly apposite. Perseverance in the light of opposition calls for courage as well as for sheer tenacity. This aspect of perseverance is highlighted in Ghandi's definition of the essence of leadership: 'To put up with misrepresentations and to stick to one's guns come what may.'

Perseverance is indeed an essential quality of leadership. Not for nothing did my old primary school have as its motto, 'Persevere'. It is the man or woman who sticks at it, who achieves the task. Nowhere is this better seen than in the life of William Carey, the great visionary and missionary pioneer, who once described himself as a 'plodder' to his nephew Eustace. 'I can plod,' he said. 'I can persevere in any definite pursuit. To this I owe everything.' What a lot the world owes to Carey because of his persevering plodding!

Humility

At first sight humility might appear to be an optional extra as far as leadership is concerned. Desirable, no doubt, yet not essential. Indeed, if anything, the very reverse would appear to be true: self-confidence, and not humility, is essential.

But, in fact, self-confidence is not necessarily the opposite of humility. Self-confidence which arises from self-awareness, as distinct from arrogance, can go hand in hand with humility. 'We are all worms,' Winston Churchill once told Lady Violet Bonham-Carter, 'but I do believe I am a glow-worm!' The humility I have in mind is not the boot-licking kind, which does indeed rob a person of all self-confidence, but rather the humility which is prepared to recognise the worth of others and to acknowledge the mistakes of self.

Dwight Eisenhower once wrote:

> A sense of humility is a quality I have observed in every leader whom I have deeply admired. I have seen Winston Churchill with humble tears of gratitude on his cheeks as he thanked people for

their help to Britain and the Allied cause. My own conviction is that every leader should have enough humility to accept, publicly, the responsibility for the mistakes of the subordinates he has himself selected and, like-wise, to give them credit, publicly, for their triumphs. I am aware that some popular theories of leadership hold that the top man must always keep his 'image' bright and shining. I believe, however, that in the long run fairness and honesty, and a generous attitude towards subordinates and associates, pays off.[20]

What is true of secular patterns of leadership is even more true of pastoral ones. Humility is a key quality for the leaders who pattern their service on that of Jesus. Thus Jack Hayward, pastor of one of America's largest Pentecostal churches, has said:

There is a desperate need for servants who will recognise their leadership role, commit themselves to it, and then get down off their pedestal and walk among the people. ... People need to know that the leader has failed on occasion, but that in his weakness he experienced the miraculous surmounting power of God.[21]

There is no place for pride in Christian service. 'Pride changed angels into devils; humility makes men into angels' (Augustine). Leaders are no different from their people as far as status is concerned. Leaders are only different from them in terms of function. In essence, however, they are 'one of them'.

Humility is important for a leader, because people follow a leader more enthusiastically when they consider his/her motives to be non-self-serving. This would, in fact, appear to have been the secret of Ho Chi Minh's army and of their twenty-five years' survival and ultimate victory in Vietnam. They were prepared to identify themselves with their men: the task was more important than any status.

There is nothing to distinguish their generals from their private soldiers except the star they wear on their collars. ... Their colonels go on foot, like privates. They live on the rice they carry on them, or the tubers they pull out of the forest earth, on the fish they catch. . . . No prepackaged rations, no cars, no fluttering pennants . . . no military bands.... But victory.[22]

Humility is of the essence of pastoral leadership. In the words of John Haggai:

Only that person who subjugates himself to the place of a servant and lets Christ continually pour his power into him is equipped to deliberately exert that special influence within a group to move it toward goals of beneficial permanence that fulfil the group's real needs.[23]

Love

Love, likewise, does not immediately come to mind when the term leadership is mentioned. Certainly love did not feature in Adair's list of attributes 'most valuable at the top level of management'. And yet if love is the key quality of the Christian life, it should not be surprising that love is the key quality in the life of the Christian leader. To paraphrase the Apostle Paul, 'without love all leading, dreaming, working, organising, delegating . . . is in vain'.

Love is vital in Christian leadership because love is the basis of all servant leadership. It was love which caused Jesus to wash his disciples' feet. It was love which gave him both the motivation and the strength to endure Gethsemane as also Calvary. Love for God reflected in love for others must form the basis of Christian service. Certainly without such love no pastor can survive ministry for any length of time. For pastoral ministry has its Gethsemanes and its Calvarys. Pastors are liable to misunderstanding and at times to rejection. Love alone enables a pastor to triumph in such situations. Without love there is bitterness. Without love there is only defeat.

Love not only initiates and sustains the service of the Christian leader, it also provides the basis for a leader's authority. Churches are voluntary associations, made up of people who have freely associated with one another. In this setting there is no place for leaders who seek to act as 'power-holders'. The authority of leaders in such a setting lies in their love for their people. It is as people begin to discover and experience his/her love for them, that they in turn allow him/her to have authority over their lives, both individually and corporately. Confidence and trust in leaders develop in proportion to the extent to which leaders are perceived to love their people.

Leaders who love their people will do their best to encourage those in their care. Such encouragement is seen as they trust them. Indeed, such trust often brings out the best in people. Encouragement is also expressed in words of appreciation for a task completed. Appreciation in turn motivates people for further service.

But along with encouragement also goes discipline. Leaders who truly love their people will be unafraid to speak the truth in love — whatever the cost of their own popularity. For without correction the life of both the individual, and also the church, may be stunted and spoiled.

Leaders who love their people will always have time for individuals. They may not be in a close relationship with everybody, but they must never be so far removed that they are not available to those who need them. Love can never be so generalised that it can never receive individual expression.

Love has no limits. Love refuses to count the cost. Leaders can never love so far, but no further — at least, not if they are patterning themselves on Jesus. In the words of Thomas à Kempis:

Love feels no burden, thinks nothing of trouble, attempts what is above its strength, pleads no excuse of impossibility; for it thinks all things lawful for itself, and all things possible. It is therefore able to undertake all things, and warrants them to take effect, where he who does not love would faint and lie down.[24]

Such love is costly. It is, however, the key to Christian leadership. It is the kind of love Jesus showed.

It was Napoleon who once said: 'Alexander, Caesar, Charlemagne, and myself founded great empires; but upon what did the creations of our genius depend? Upon force. Jesus alone founded his empire upon love, and to this very day millions would die for him.' It is the kind of love which Jesus displayed which leaders are called to emulate. Such love will prove effective in achieving the task, building the team, and meeting the needs of individuals.

4. Graces first then gifts

A comparison between Adair's list of qualities needed for secular leadership with the subsequent lists of qualities needed for pastoral leadership is instructive. In the former the emphasis is on ability, whereas in the latter the emphasis is on character. Clearly ability is important for those who lead the people of God, but at the end of the day it is not all-important. Character, too, counts.

This emphasis on 'graces' rather than 'gifts' is also present in Paul's list of qualities necessary for leadership (1 Tim 3:2–7). Thus when Paul wrote to Timothy, his chief concern was that the life of the Christian leader should be exemplary as far as the world was concerned: 'Now the overseer must be above reproach' (1 Tim 3:2). It is under this general umbrella that Paul then listed a further eleven virtues that should characterise any Christian leader: 'the husband of but one wife' (ie, marital fidelity), 'temperate', 'self-controlled', 'respectable', 'hospitable', 'able to teach' (this is the one item on the list that specifies an ability), 'not given to much wine', 'not violent but gentle', 'not quarrelsome', and 'not a lover of money'. Paul then added that the leader must have an exemplary family, and must not be a new convert. He sums the list up with the necessity of the leader having 'a good reputation with outsiders'.

From the point of view of a person writing a book on

pastoral leadership, Paul's list of qualities needed by an aspiring leader is somewhat disappointing. For with one exception ('able to teach'), Paul tells us nothing of what a leader might be expected to do. But on reflection this emphasis on behaviour is healthy and necessary not least for those who would serve in today's moral climate. The life of the Christian leader must be a testimony to the power of the gospel. A person may have all the gifts imaginable, yet if there is moral failure, then the gospel is denied before it is even preached. Here then is a challenge to theological colleges to ensure that the candidates they accept have not only gifts, but also graces. Their character, their personality, the way they relate to people — these things count as much as how they can perform in the pulpit! For leaders, if they are going to be effective in their ministry, must in the first place live lives that reflect the King whom they serve. In other words, the emphasis is on what they are, and not just on what they do. It is to this particular quality that we will now turn in the final chapter.

Notes

1. John Adair, *Effective Leadership* (Pan Business/Management: London, 1983), pp 12–13.
2. Charles Simpson, article in *Pastoral Renewal*, vol 10, (December 1986), pp 8–15.
3. Peter Wagner, *Leading Your Church to Growth* (Regal: Ventura, CA, 1984), p 169 ff.
4. J Oswald Sanders, *Spiritual Leadership* (Marshalls: London, 1967), pp 23–24.
5. Ted Engstrom, *The Making of a Christian Leader* (Zondervan, Grand Rapids, MI, 1976), pp 88–89.
6. J Oswald Sanders, *op cit*, p 24.
7. John Haggai, *Lead On* (Word: Waco, TX, 1986), p ix.
8. Ronald Knox, *Enthusiasm* (Oxford University Press: Oxford, 1950), p 591.
9. Robert Schuller, *Your Church Has Real Possibilities* (Regal: Glendale, CA, 1974), p 87.

10. Quoted by John Adair, *op cit*, p 185.
11. Ted Engstrom, *The Pursuit of Excellence* (Zondervan: Grand Rapids, MI, 1982), p 57.
12. John Perry, *Christian Leadership* (Hodder and Stoughton: London, 1983), p 9.
13. Quoted by John Stott, *Issues Facing Christians Today* (Marshalls: Basingstoke, 1984), p 332.
14. *Ibid*, p 331.
15. Quoted by John Adair, *op cit*, p 117.
16. Robert Roxburgh, *Renewal Down to Earth* (Kingsway: Eastbourne, 1987), p 110.
17. John Stott, *op cit*, p 332.
18. Peter Wagner, *op cit*, p 103.
19. Paul Beasley-Murray and Alan Wilkinson, *Turning the Tide* (Bible Society: London, 1981), p 34.
20. Quoted by John Adair, *op cit*, p 57.
21. Quoted by Peter Wagner, *op cit*, p 84.
22. J Roy, quoted by Phillip King, *Leadership Explosion* (Hodder and Stoughton: London, 1987), p 127.
23. John Haggai, *op cit*, p 71.
24. Thomas à Kempis, *The Imitation of Christ*, III 5.

IO

The Leader: The Vital Relationship

1. A call to be men and women of God

God's men and women

Gifts and graces, qualities of every kind are necessary in the pastoral leader, who will work as a senior partner with others, to achieve the task, build the team and meet the needs of individuals.

However, there is one qualification with which we have not dealt. If pastors are to be successful in their role as leaders, they need to be God's men and women.

From one point of view all God's people are called to be men and women of God. Spirituality is not an extra for some. There are no first and second-class citizens of God. In one sense the clergy-laity divide of the Old Covenant has been removed. The priesthood of all believers is a reality.

None of this can be denied. And yet, there is also a sense in which Christian leaders in particular need to be men and women of God.

It is instructive to look at the way in which the term 'man of God' is used in the Scriptures. In the Old Testament the expression is used of some of the great servants of God: Moses (Deut 33:1; Josh 14:6); Samuel (1 Sam 9:6); David (Neh 12:24); Elijah (1 Kings 17:18), and Elisha (2 Kings 4:7) are all called 'men of God'. In the New Testament the expression occurs only twice: on the first occasion (1 Tim 6:11) it explicitly refers to Timothy; on the second occasion (2 Tim 3:17) it implicitly refers to Timothy as 'the minister of the word of God'.[1] JND Kelly therefore concludes: 'It connotes one who is in God's service and speaks in his name and admirably fits one who is a pastor.'[2]

In 1 Timothy 6:11–12, Timothy, as a 'man of God', is commanded to 'flee' from sin and 'pursue righteousness, godliness, faith, love, endurance and gentleness'. A little earlier Paul commands Timothy to 'set an example for the believers in speech, in life, in love, in faith and in purity' (1 Tim 4:12). The 'man of God', precisely because he is a 'man of God', is expected to set an example to others in his flock. Thus Lesslie Newbigin has written: 'A true Christian pastor will be one who can dare to say to his people: "Follow me, as I am following Jesus." That is a terrible test for any pastor. A true pastor must have such a relationship with Jesus and his people that he follows Jesus and they follow him.'[3]

This is indeed a 'terrible test'. It is a terrible responsibility. It is only natural for pastors to fight against such a calling, for they know they are only human. But it is a calling they cannot escape. Pastoral leadership involves leadership by example. 'People don't do what a pastor tells them to do,' it has been said, 'they watch what he does and then copy it.' All the more reason therefore for pastors to practise what they preach (see Matthew 23:2–3).

A call to be

The call to pastoral leadership, therefore, is in the first place a call to be, rather than a call to do. In this respect Paul Fiddes is right when he maintains: 'An office of leadership is indeed a function within ministry, but it functions first of all in giving a place where someone can learn to be. Because the office is there, because Christ calls a person to it, it provides an opportunity for him to learn to be with Christ, for Christ, in himself and for others.'[4] Or in the words of Henri

Nouwen: 'Ministry is not an eight-to-five job, but primarily a way of life, which is for others to see and understand so that liberation can become a possibility. ... Ordination means the recognition and affirmation of the fact that a man ... lives in intimate contact with the God of the living, and has a burning desire to show others the way to him.'[5] This may sound strange to some Protestant ears. Are pastors priests? In one sense, yes of course they are. They represent God to their fellow men and women. True, this is no exclusive priesthood, for other Christians may share in it. But it is a vital part of their ministry.

It is in their relationship with God that the authority of leaders is to be found. They are but under-shepherds. Therefore if they are to tend the flock of God, in the first instance they must be followers. It is not accidental that in John 20:19 the call to follow comes after the call to tend the flock. Pastoral leaders have authority in so far as they are 'under' God's authority (see Charles Sibthorpe, *A Man under Authority* [Kingsway: Eastbourne, 1984], p 19: 'As God works *in* you, he will be able to work *through* you').

Pastors therefore have no option but to major on their relationship with God. This relationship is primary. Neglect of this relationship negates ministry. Pastors need to heed the words of Ann Shields: 'God looks for more from us than strategies for church renewal, first-rate preaching, creative evangelistic approaches, sound theology and biblical study, or responsible involvement in social issues. ... He wants each of us to have our lives in his order.' She quotes the prayer of John Henry Newman: 'Shine in me and so be in me that all with whom I come in contact may know thy presence in my soul. Let them look up and see no longer me but Jesus.' She goes on:

A statement attributed to various famous preachers paints a vivid image of what we must be: 'I should be so on fire with the Holy Spirit that when I step into the pulpit, people watch me burn.' Is that too poetic? Or is it simply what God wants to do with us? The times require a holy people, and, therefore, holy leaders.[6]

2. Look to Jesus

How many pastors fulfil their calling to be men and women of God? I suggest a looking in three directions. In the first place, pastors need to be 'looking to Jesus the pioneer' (Heb 12:2, RSV). The words of William Temple, when enthroned Bishop of Manchester, need to be repeated by pastors whenever they are inducted to a particular pastoral charge:

> I come as a learner, with no policy to advocate, no plan already formed to follow. But I come with one burning desire: it is that in all our activities, sacred and secular and ecclesiastical and social, we should help each other fix our eyes on Jesus, making him our only guide. . . . Pray for me, I ask you, not chiefly that I may be wise and strong, or any such thing, though for these things I need your prayers. But pray for me chiefly, that I may never let go of the unseen hand of the Lord Jesus and may live in daily fellowship with him. It is so that you will most of all help me to help you.

'Looking unto Jesus.' This, the motto of the Crusaders' Union, should be the motto of every pastor.

For example

Jesus has given the pattern for 'ministry', a pattern of service. Indeed, the very word 'ministry' means service. Jesus said that the leader should become 'as one who serves. . . . I am among you as one who serves' (Lk 22:26–27, RSV). John Mott, commenting on these verses, defined leadership as 'rendering the maximum of service . . .; the largest unselfishness . . .; unwearying and unceasing absorption in the greatest work of the world, the building up of the Kingdom of our Lord Jesus Christ'.[7]

The pattern of service Jesus has given is the pattern of

sacrifice: 'The Son of Man *also* came not to be served but to serve, and to give his life as a ransom for many' (Mk 10:45, RSV, my italics). The 'good shepherd' who 'lays down his life for the sheep' (Jn 10:11) is the one who calls his followers to lay down their lives for one another (Jn 15:12–13; see 1 John 3:16). This is the context, and not simply that of footwashing, in which Jesus says: 'I have given you an example, that you also should do as I have done to you' (Jn 13:15, RSV).

Look to Jesus — and not to others. For Jesus is the ultimate role model. Inevitably, at the beginning of their ministries, younger pastors tend to look to more experienced and more 'successful' pastors. No doubt there is much to be gained from learning from others. But ultimately such models disappoint. For even the finest of leaders are but human and fallible. Jesus alone is the infallible model.

'Look to Jesus,' writes the unknown author of the Letter to the Hebrews. The words that follow, though written with Christians generally in mind, surely have a special significance for leaders: look to Jesus, 'the author and perfecter of our faith, who for the joy set before him endured the cross, scorning the shame. ... Consider him who endured such opposition from sinful men, so that you will not grow weary and lose heart' (Heb 12:2–3). Life can be tough for the Christian leader. There can be misunderstanding, opposition, loneliness, pain. But all these things and more Jesus experienced. Look to him, and gain fresh inspiration for the fray. 'Christ suffered for you,' wrote Peter, 'leaving you an example, that you should follow in his steps' (1 Pet 2:21). Suffering precedes resurrection. Not even the Christian leader is exempt from cross-bearing. Therefore, 'Keep ever before you the likeness of Christ crucified. As you meditate on the life of Jesus Christ, you should grieve that you have not tried more earnestly to conform yourself to him.'[8]

The example of Jesus is not limited to a readiness to suffer. Michael Griffiths lists, in addition to this readiness to suffer, six other qualities found in Christ which the Scriptures emphasise we should reflect: a readiness to serve (Mk 10:45; Phil 2:5–7), a readiness to obey (Phil 2:7, 12–14; Heb 5:7–9), and the qualities of patience (Heb 12:2–3; 1 Tim 1:16), gentleness (2 Cor 10:1), humility (Phil 2:3,8) and love (Eph 5:1–2).[9] None of these qualities is to be peculiar to leaders — they are to be the hallmark of Christian living. But what a difference it makes when they too characterise Christian leadership. Would that all leaders could say with Mr Standfast of John Bunyan's *Pilgrim's Progress*: 'Wherever I have seen the print of his shoe on earth, there I have coveted to set my foot too.'

For strength

Pastoral ministry can be a draining business. It involves a constant self-giving to other people — whether through preaching, through counselling, through empathising with people as they go through the crises of life, or whether through the general 'wear and tear' of giving leadership. How necessary therefore it is for leaders to look to Jesus for spiritual renewal. To open up themselves to his life-giving and life-sustaining presence. To so 'abide in him' that the branches draw fresh sap from the vine. Only in this way can new strength be found to love and to serve.

John Perry makes the insightful comment:

The hardest lesson to accept and learn about Christian leadership is that it has to be in God's strength and not our own. Other qualifications for leadership are necessary, but the primary qualification is a recognition that God's work has to be done in his way and with his power. This cuts across the accepted attitude, 'I can do this in my own strength'.[10]

The fact is that ministry can often be sustained in the first few years by natural talent. But there comes a point when natural talent no longer suffices. Indeed, natural talent can prove a stumbling-block to the operation of God's power in our lives. Sometimes it takes a real crisis in ministry to realise that the true source of power is in our utter dependence on Christ. This was certainly Paul's experience. When tormented almost to the point of distraction by his 'thorn in the flesh', he discovered the truth of the risen Christ: 'My grace is sufficient for you, for my power is made perfect in weakness' (2 Cor 12:9). Paul's weakness was a condition of his experiencing God's power. Self-confidence only acts as a block to the source of divine power.

Strength to minister in Christ's name is found in Christ alone. Our own resources are finite, his are infinite. This was the experience of Carlo Caretto who, in his *Letters from the Desert*, described how God made him face up to his inadequacy and his need of power greater than his own:

> Now I contrast my powerlessness with the powerfulness of God, the heap of my sins with the completeness of his mercy. And I place the abyss of my smallness beneath the abyss of his greatness. God can do everything and I can do nothing, but if I offer this nothing in prayer to God, everything becomes possible to me.[11]

Strength is needed in time of weakness. Strength is also needed in time of temptation. As with all God's people, the temptations that afflict leaders can be many and various. 'Success' in the ministry can be a leader's downfall. Thus according to CH Spurgeon:

> Success exposes a man to the pressures of people and thus tempts him to hold on to his gains by means of fleshly methods and practices, and to let himself be ruled wholly by the dictatorial demands of incessant expansion. Success can go to my head and will unless I remember that it is God who accomplishes the work, that he can continue to do so without my help, and that he will be able to make out with other means whenever he wants to cut me out.

In such circumstances leaders need to look to Jesus for strength to remain both humble and faithful.

Equally demanding are those occasions when 'success' does not appear to accompany one's ministry. The temptation is then to look around, and in looking around become jealous of others. Indeed, in may ways jealousy seems to be the ministerial sin *par excellence*. Michael Ramsey writes that jealousy:

> is a poison which spreads more easily than you would think. You can be jealous of a man because he has gifts which you would like. You can be jealous of a man because while you think he lacks your gifts, he seems to be more successful than you. You can be jealous of a man because some of the people look to him when you thought of them as your people looking to you for spiritual help. .... Thus complex are the elements which create pastoral jealousy.[12]

All the more reason, therefore, to look to Jesus for strength to serve.

For direction

Herodotus once claimed that the most bitter sorrow is to aspire to do much and then to achieve nothing. However, in fact the most bitter sorrow is to aspire to do much, and to do it, and then to discover that it was not worth doing!

Leadership is not about going in any direction. It is about going in the right direction, in the direction that God wants for our lives. Hence the need for leaders to make time every day to reflect prayerfully on the past, review the present and seek God's will for the future.

Charles Hummel wrote about the problem of distinguishing between the important and the urgent:

> The important task rarely must be done today, or even this week. .... But the urgent tasks call for instant action ... endless demands pressure every hour and day. ... The momentary appeal of these tasks seems irresistible and important and they devour our energy. But in the light of time's perspective their deceptive prominence fades; with a sense of loss we recall the

important tasks pushed aside again. We realise we've become slaves to the tyranny of the urgent.

What is the solution to this familiar problem? Hummel suggests a daily seeking of God's will, as Jesus sought God's will: 'By this means he warded off the urgent and accomplished the important. It gave him a sense of direction, set a steady pace, and enabled him to do every task God had assigned him.'[13]

Jesus has an individual plan, not only for our lives, but also for the lives of churches. What he may want to do in one place, he may not want to do in another. It is only as leaders look to Jesus — and not to other leaders — that they discover his direction for the people he has put in their charge. 'Lord, what about him?' asked Peter, referring to John. Jesus answered, 'What is that to you? You must follow me' (Jn 21:21–22). Comparison with others is not the point: following Jesus is the issue. Leaders need to learn that every church has its own unique personality, and that it takes all kinds of churches if the gospel is to pervade every level of society. 'These differences are not weaknesses of the church; they are deep strengths,' writes David Womack, 'that prove the message of Christ is applicable to any group of people on the face of the earth.'[14]

Following Jesus involves working his way. DT Niles, the Methodist leader from Sri Lanka, used the following picture to describe the need for leaders to learn the way of Christ:

If you are working on a piece of wood, you must work according to the grain; otherwise you will only get splinters. We are not free. There is a grain in the universe; there is a grain in history; there is a grain in the church, because God is at work. And if we do not gather with him, however wonderful our plans, however ardently we labour, however carefully we work, the result of it all is scattering, not gathering (see Matthew 12:30; Luke 11:23).

3. Look to yourselves

Men and women of God not only need to look to Jesus, but also to themselves. 'Watch your life and doctrine,' (1 Tim 4:16) wrote Paul to Timothy. 'Keep watch over yourselves' was his exhortation to the Ephesian elders at Miletus (Acts 20:28). For men and women there can never be room for complacency.

In some ways Paul was only echoing the book of Proverbs: 'Above all else, guard your heart, for it is the wellspring of your life' (Prov 4:23). 'Action is the stream,' wrote Thomas Merton, 'and contemplation is the spring.' But what happens if the spring dries up? All the more need to 'guard the heart', for it is the 'wellspring' of one's life.

The Apostle Paul spoke of the Christian life — and of the preacher's life in particular — as involving self-discipline: 'I do not run like a man running aimlessly; I do not fight like a man beating in the air. No, I beat my body and make it my slave so that after I have preached to others, I myself will not be disqualified for the prize' (1 Cor 9:26–27). Richard Baxter of Kidderminster took up the theme:

> See that the work of saving grace is thoroughly wrought in your own souls. Take heed to yourselves, lest you be void of that saving grace of God which you offer to others and be strangers to the effectual working of that Gospel which you preach; lest while you proclaim the necessity of a Saviour to the world, your own heart should neglect him and his saving benefits. Take heed to yourselves, lest you perish while you call upon others to take heed of the perishing; lest you famish yourselves while you prepare their food.

Pastors must constantly be working at their relationship with God. This was Robert Murray M'Cheyne's point when with Isaiah 49:2 ('he made my mouth like a sharpened sword') in mind he exhorted: 'Do not forget the culture of the inner man — I mean of the heart. How diligently the cavalry officer keeps his sabre clean and sharp; every stain he rubs off with the greatest care. Remember you are God's sword. A holy minister is an aweful weapon in the hand of God.'

Abiding in Christ

Leaders are almost by definition activists. There are tasks to be achieved, a team to be built, needs of individuals crying out for attention. Yet the message of John 15 is clear: activity is useless unless counterbalanced by an abiding in Christ. 'Abide in me, and I in you ... for apart from me you can do nothing' (Jn 15:4–5, RSV).

'Beware of the barrenness of a busy life' was the constant refrain of Bishop J Taylor Smith. No doubt these words are applicable to people in general, but are they not applicable in particular to pastors? It has been said, 'Being a shepherd isn't the same as being a sheepdog. Caring for people doesn't mean fussing around them in the morning hours, when a man should be in his study — on his knees.'

However much pastors feel themselves under pressure, with so many things to do, so many people to see, so many meetings to attend, the discipline of the spiritual life needs to be maintained. Jesus had enormous pressures on him during his three years of public ministry, yet he maintained a relationship with his Father that daily sustained and renewed him. Whether early in the morning or late in the evening he made time to withdraw. If daily withdrawal was a top priority for Jesus, then how much more it should be for those who are his followers, and especially for those who lead in his name.

Driven or called?

Gordon MacDonald makes much of the distinction between people who are 'driven' and people who are 'called'. In his definition, a driven person

is most often gratified only by accomplishment ... is pre-occupied with the symbols of accomplishment ... is usually caught in the controlled pursuit of expansion ... tends to have a limited regard for integrity ... often possesses limited or undeveloped people skills ... tends to be highly competitive ... often possesses a volcanic force of anger ... is usually abnormally busy.

In the light of this he asks: 'Are we driven people, propelled by the winds of our times, pressed to conform or compete? Or are we called people, the recipients of the gracious beckoning of Christ when He promises to make us into something?'[15] A sobering question! If the truth be told, all too many of us need to organise our private world in a better way. We need to make better use of our time. We need to 'look to ourselves' and become more self-disciplined.

Making time ...

If leaders are to be men and women of God, they will need to make time for God. They will need to schedule time for God into their diaries as much as they might schedule in an appointment with one of their church members. What is more, once that appointment has been made, it then needs to be held to, unless a crisis demands otherwise. Leaders do their people a service by being absent from them, as well as being present with them — particularly when that absence means that they are present with their God. It takes a degree of self-discipline not to be at the beck and call of others, but in fact such discipline is ultimately a service to people rather than a disservice.

Henri Nouwen underlines this point:

When someone says, 'The minister is unavailable because this is his day of solitude, this is his day in the hermitage, this is his desert day,' could that not be a consoling ministry? What it says is that the minister is unavailable to me, not because he is more available to others, but because he is with God, and God alone — the God who is our God.[16]

... to be still before the Lord

It is only as we still our hearts and minds that we can look to Jesus, find inspiration from his example, strength from his presence, and direction from his leading.

Leaders need to learn the secret of 'abiding' in Jesus. Abiding should contain no strain or effort: it is rest from effort. The natural branch should not strain to remain a part of the vine; it simply is. All it need do is to stay connected. 'Abiding,' wrote Thomas Merton, 'is a consciousness of our union with God, of our complete dependence on Him, for all our vital acts in the spiritual life, and of His constant, loving presence in the depth of our souls.' In other words, amid all the stresses and strains of pastoral life, it is good — indeed, it is vital — to practise 'the presence of God' and in doing so to be renewed in spirit and in mind.

God needs to be found, but he cannot be found in the noise and restlessness of life. 'God,' said Mother Teresa, 'is the friend of silence. See how nature — trees, flowers, grass — grow in silence; see the stars, the moon and sun, how they move in silence. ... The more we receive in silent prayer, the more we can give in our active life. We need silence in order to be able to touch souls.'[17]

The Twenty-third Psalm for Busy People, which World Vision use to preface their manual on Time Management, expresses the difference to life when we are still and wait on God:

> The Lord is my pace-setter, I shall not rush,
> He makes me stop and rest for quiet intervals,
> He provides me with images of stillness,
> which restore my serenity.
> He leads me in the ways of effectiveness
> through calmness of mind,
> and His guidance is peace.
> Even though I have a great many things to accomplish
> today, I will not fret for His presence is here,
> His timelessness, His all-importance will keep me
> in balance.

He prepares refreshment and renewal in the midst of
my activity by anointing my mind with his oils of
tranquillity,
My cup of joyous energy overflows.
Surely harmony and effectiveness shall be the fruit
of my hours,
for I shall walk at the pace of my Lord,
and dwell in His house for ever.

... *to read his word*

Leaders need to read God's word not just for the purposes
of sermon preparation, but also for the good of their own
souls. They also need to be fed by the 'Bread of Life'.
Dietrich Bonhoeffer firmly believed in steeping himself in
God's word:

Every day in which I do not penetrate more deeply into the
knowledge of God's Word in Holy Scripture is a lost day for me.
I can only move forward with certainty upon the firm ground of
the Word of God. ... I cannot expound the Scripture for others
if I do not let it speak daily to me. I will misuse the Word in my
office as a preacher if I do not continue to meditate upon it in
prayer.[18]

Bonhoeffer was a great advocate of meditation on Scripture.
However, along with meditation goes study. The two need
not be mutually contradictory. Indeed, the more we dig deep
into God's word, the more we find. A great theologian of
former days, Sir Edwyn Hoskyns, once said of his own
studies that 'he began with his head in a lexicon and ended at
the throne of God'.

Leaders need to continue to grow and develop in the faith.
Thus Roy Oswald has written:

In our Alban Institute study of long pastorates (ten or more
years) lay people's most frequent complaint was that their pastor
had become ingrown and stale. We concluded that it is more
difficult to maintain vitality in a long pastorate than in a short

one. The key to vitality is a pastor who consistently gives attention to his/her spiritual growth. The way to keep a congregation vital and growing is to be a vital, growing person in their midst.[19]

Pastoral ministry calls for development, it calls for progess (see 1 Timothy 4:15). One way of stimulating such growth and development is by taking God's word seriously and actually reading it!

... to pray

Michael Ramsey wrote of the necessity for the priest to be 'a man of prayer': 'As the teacher of theology the priest must pray, as theology which is alive includes not only book work, but the authentic knowledge of God which comes through prayer alone.'[20] From a different angle, James Stewart emphasises the importance of prayer for the preacher:

How shall any man be strong to do Christ's work today, with the purposefulness and passion and mastery of life that shine on every page of the Gospels, if he neglects Christ's hidden secret? Chalmers was indeed going to the root of the matter when he declared that most failures in the ministry were due, not to lack of visiting or of study or of organisational activity, but to lack of prayer.[21]

Prayer is of the essence of the Christian life. It is of the essence of the leader's life. Prayer not only through which they cultivate their relationship with God, but also through which they intercede for others, not least for those for whom they are responsible. Is not praying for one's people part of what is involved in keeping watch over the flock (Heb 13:17)? Leaders need to pray for their people. As they mention before the Lord the names of those in their charge, they will no doubt visualise them, and think of their work, their difficulties and their temptations. In the words of Michael Ramsey, they will be like 'Aaron of old who went into the holy of holies wearing a breastplate with jewels representing the tribes of Israel whose priest he was: he went near to God with the people on his heart'.[22] Like Paul, leaders will not cease to pray for the churches in their care (see Colossians 1:9). What a difference such prayer can make to preaching! What a difference such prayer can make to pastoral care too!

Such praying is not always easy. But then Paul's injunction — 'And pray in the Spirit on all occasions with all kinds of prayers and requests. With this in mind, be alert and always keep on praying for all the saints' (Eph 6:18) — comes in a context where Paul has asserted that 'our struggle is not against flesh and blood, but against the rulers, against the authorities, against the powers of this dark world and against the spiritual forces of evil in the heavenly realms' (Eph 6:12). The clear implication is that prayer is a vital element in the spiritual battle — indeed, *the* vital element!

... to relax

Relaxing is also part of being a man or woman of God! To be a person of compassion is not necessarily to be strung out by every human need that comes along. Sometimes 'no' needs to be said in order that caring can continue. The Greeks had a proverb: 'The bow that is always bent (ie, always stretched taut) will soon cease to shoot straight.'

Here the example of Jesus is surely significant. For on one occasion notable for its busyness — Mark records that 'so many people were coming and going that they did not even have a chance to eat' — Jesus said to his disciples, 'Come with me by yourselves to a quiet place and get some rest' (Mk 6:31). In this passage Jesus exemplifies not only a doctrine of work, but also a doctrine of rest! To paraphrase the words of the Preacher: 'There is a time for everything. . . . A time to work, and a time not to work!'

Roy Oswald has pictured the time available to pastors as a triangle, the three 'points' indicating parish ministry, spiritual formation, and family/rest/relaxation. Each angle is important. Only when the three points are correctly angled is wholeness to be found.[23]

Relaxation needs to be viewed as a discipline. It is part of God's order for mankind that one day in seven should be set aside for rest. God's order should be respected. Admittedly this is an effort for conscientious pastors — the demands of their ministry are insatiable. Yet, as I have sought to argue, they are not alone in ministry. They are surrounded by a team with whom leadership and service may be shared. Let the church be the church instead of being dependent on one person. God, it has been said, does not want us to be married to the church — that's adultery (the church is already married)!

Honesty acknowledges that crises arise and there are times when a day off proves impossible. All the more reason, therefore, to ensure that the pastor is compensated. Busy pastors — for their own sake, for the sake of their families, and ultimately for the sake of their churches — need to ensure that regular holidays are built into their diaries. Holidays at least are more difficult to disturb. Not only should a week be taken off after Christmas and Easter respectively, but pastors should unashamedly take off a further four weeks in the summer!

4. Look for friends

Some years ago Mrs Norah Coggan, the wife of the (then) Archbishop of Canterbury, gave an address to clergy wives entitled 'Who helps the Helpers?' The title was taken from one of Juvenal's satires. Juvenal literally said, 'Who is to guard the guards themselves? Who is to watch over those who are doing the watching?' In its original context, this had something to do with a woman who comes to entice the guard. However, the quotation is capable of more general application, and Mrs Coggan applied it in particular to those involved in pastoral work. 'The time comes,' she said, 'when we [the helpers] have lifted too many burdens and we really are worn down, exhausted and depressed. Maybe our faith is cold and also our lives and witness for the Lord. Perhaps we feel we are in a dark tunnel. Depression comes over us. What then?'

What then indeed. The fact is that not even leaders can go it alone. However much they may seek to look to Jesus and to look to themselves, ultimately they discover that there is a need for friends. Friends who will help them through the dark and difficult patches of pastoral ministry. Friends who will strengthen their hand in God (see 1 Samuel 22:15).

Partners in life

For those of us who are married, we can and should turn for help to our life partners. That's surely where, in the first instance, mutual comfort and help are to be found.

The words of Ecclesiastes 4:9–10 and 12 come to mind: 'Two are better than one. . . . If one falls down, his friend can help him up. But pity the man who falls and has no-one to help him up! . . . One may be overpowered, two can defend themselves.' These words can be applied to married life in general, but they can also be applied to life in the manse in particular.

And yet there are times when partners in life cannot help. It is not that they do not care, but rather they care too much. They, perhaps even more acutely than their spouses, feel hurt and pain. In this not infrequent situation, both are in need of help and support. Together they need to find others who can help them through their crisis.

Friends in the church

Traditionally ministerial friendships within the church have been frowned on. In days gone by, at least, prospective pastors have been told in their theological colleges that they should have no friends in the church. Needless to say, there was good reason for such advice. There is no doubt that the making of close friends within a church can cause problems. It is easy for people to feel 'hurt' because they have been left out of the inner circle. Members of the congregation begin to think that the pastor and his spouse have their 'favourites'.

Yet for all the undoubted dangers and difficulties, the advice that is now given in theological colleges is changing. People are beginning to realise that pastors and their partners cannot be expected to go it alone. Or, if they do, then there are going to be casualties within their ranks.

Provided people are circumspect in the way in which they conduct their friendships — at all church services and activities they should be available to all — then such friendships should be encouraged. Indeed, such friendships can not only meet the social needs of the couple in the manse, but also their spiritual needs. Some of the friendships may even develop into a kind of 'spiritual growth group' for pastors and their spouses, where true openness and honesty can prevail in a way which would not be possible in any other group within the church. Within the confidence of such a group, encouragement might be given, but also on occasion an element of discipline might be practised. Why should the family in the manse be removed from pastoral care?

Howard Clinebell describes the kind of relationships I have in mind: 'Growth stimulating relationships are warm, caring and trustful, at the same time they are honest, confronting, and open. Caring + confrontation = growth. This is the growth formula.'[24] Clinebell is speaking of growth groups generally. But surely this can be applied to the special kind of group in which the pastors and their partners are involved? For they too need to grow. They too need to be in the kind of relationship where on the one hand they can be cared for, but on the other hand they can be confronted. This relationship is best offered by just one or two couples within a church.

Friends outside the church

Wise pastors and their partners will seek to make and maintain friendships outside the church. Here I have in mind not so much 'secular' friendships, although they have their place, but rather the developing of friendships with other like-minded couples with whom the ups and downs of pastoral ministry can be shared. Such 'peer' relationships can form an essential safety-valve to pastoral ministry. For within the security of such friendship, hair can be let down, tops can be blown, and sorrows and joys can be shared. Such friendships can provide a form for fun; they also can provide a form for prayer.

'Very Resourceful People'

'Very Resourceful People' is the term Gordon MacDonald uses for those who 'ignite our passion for faith and for Christlike performance'.[25] The terms people use to describe such VRPs vary from 'soul friend' to 'spiritual director' to 'father or mother in God'. The reference here is not so much to a 'peer', but rather to someone who is perceived to be slightly further ahead in the spiritual pilgrimage. When the ashes, as it were, have clogged the fire, they can often be helpful in 'poking around' so that the stifling elements are removed and thereby enabling fresh fuel to be taken aboard.

Needless to say, such VRPs cannot live the Christian life for us. We have to make our own pilgrimage. As Anne Long rightly says, 'A spiritual director is not a problem-solver to whom we run for infallible answers. We are to work out our own salvation, and Christian discipleship is not a collecting of recipes from others for instant sanctification.'[26] Nonetheless, they have often been that way before, and can be of immense help in enabling pastors to develop in their Christian life.

'Very Important People'

The 'Very Important People' are our peers. On the one hand they can be a group of fellow pastors (a 'fraternal') from whom support and encouragement for ministry can be found. Whether formally or informally constituted, every pastor needs to be within such a network of supportive friendship.

On the other hand, VIPs can be found within the church. They may be fellow elders or deacons. They are those with whom the leadership is shared. Here, too, support and encouragement can be found. Just as Aaron and Hur held up Moses' hands and supported him in prayer (Exod 17:12), so too the leaders of the church are called to surround their pastor with prayerful support. Denis Duncan made the interesting comment:

> The development of the congregation as 'the agent of mission' needs a team at its centre in which the members relate to each other at deep levels. The early church had 'all things in common'. It was thinking of possessions, but it may be that the sharing that phrase represents at a 'material' level is equally appropriate at emotional and spiritual levels. ... If the church is going to go forward with an effective evangelism, those who are leaders in the work — the ministers — must be looked after in terms of their spiritual and emotional needs.[27]

In other words, pastors need to be pastored, and in the first instance this is the responsibility of the elders or deacons or whatever the leadership structure is.

There is then a whole variety of networks of supportive relationships to which pastors and their partners can turn. Probably at differing times in their ministries different groups will be of particular significance and help to them.

It is important to note that such support systems are not luxuries in the pastoral life. They are essential for growth and development — indeed, at times they are essential for survival. Time therefore needs to be given to maintain such relationships. However, provided such groups are truly honest, open and supportive, the cost is more than worth while.

5. The vital relationship

We return to where we began. The prime qualification for a leader within the context of a church is to be a man or woman of God. Only so can the task be achieved, the team be built, and the needs of individuals be met. To be men and women of God, however, demands that leaders work constantly at their relationship with their Lord.

Thus, according to Acts 6:3, a key qualification for Christian leadership is to be 'full of the Spirit'. But as Paul reminds the Ephesians, 'fullness' is not a one-off experience: we must 'keep on being filled with God's Spirit' (Eph 5:18). There is no standing still in the Christian life. Leaders cannot rest secure on their past experiences of God. This is well illustrated by DL Moody's reply to the question, had he been filled with the Spirit? 'Yes,' he said, 'but I leak.' In other words, our spiritual life must be constantly renewed.

But renewal is not sufficient. The leader's spiritual life needs to be constantly deepened. Progress needs to be made in the Christian life. The picture of the river of life in Ezekiel 47, which became ever deeper, can perhaps be seen as a symbol of our experience of God. Our experience of God is not to remain static, rather we are to go on. And in going on, leaders will be able to lead their people ever deeper in the things of God. 'Leaders,' Charles Sibthorpe has written, 'live under the responsibility of continually pressing on with God. This is not to say that every leader will be a spiritual giant: you need only be half a pace in front of the people.'[28] Nonetheless, this is still an awesome responsibility. All the more need, therefore, for Christian leaders to cultivate their relationship with God!

In conclusion

> Do not pray for easy lives;
> pray to be stronger people!
> Do not pray for tasks equal to your powers;
> pray for powers equal to your tasks.
> Then the doing of your work shall be no miracle,
> but you shall be a miracle.
> Every day you shall wonder at yourself,

at the richness of life which has come to you
by the grace of God.

Philips Brooks

Notes

1. Gordon Fee, *1 and 2 Timothy, Titus* (Harper and Row: San Francisco, 1984), p 108.
2. JND Kelly, *The Pastoral Epistles* (A and C Black: London, 1972), p 139.
3. Lesslie Newbigin, *The Good Shepherd* (Mowbray: Oxford, 1985), p 14.
4. Paul Fiddes, *A Leading Question* (Baptist Union: London), p 24.
5. Henri Nouwen, *Creative Ministry* (Doubleday: New York, 1978), p 108.
6. Ann Shields, article in *Pastoral Renewal* (November 1986), p 14.
7. J Oswald Sanders, *Spiritual Leadership* (Marshalls: London, 1967), p 25.
8. Thomas à Kempis, *The Imitation of Christ* I 25.
9. Michael Griffiths, *The Example of Jesus* (Hodder and Stoughton: London, 1985), pp 89–103.
10. John Perry, *Christian Leadership* (Hodder and Stoughton: London, 1983), pp 10–11.
11. *Ibid*, p 11.
12. Michael Ramsey, *The Christian Priest Today* (SPCK: London, 1985), pp 71–72.
13. Charles Hummel, 'The Tyranny of the Urgent', *Christian Arena* (March 1985), p 2 ff.
14. David Womack, *The Pyramid Principle of Church Growth* (Bethany: Minneapolis, MN, 1977), p 41.
15. Gordon MacDonald, *Ordering Your Private World* (Highland Books: Crowborough, East Sussex, 1985), pp 10, 33.
16. Henri Nouwen, *The Living Reminder* (Gill and MacMillan: Dublin, 1977), p 49.
17. Malcolm Muggeridge, *Something Beautiful for God* (Fount: London, 1972).
18. Dietrich Bonhoeffer, *Meditating on the Word* (Cowley: Cambridge, Massachusetts, 1986), pp 30–31.

19. Roy Oswald, *Clergy Stress* (Alban Institute: Washington DC, 1982), p 55.
20. Michael Ramsey, *op cit*, p 9.
21. James Stewart, *Preaching* (Hodder and Stoughton: London, 1955), p 176.
22. Michael Ramsey, *op cit*, p 15.
23. Roy Oswald, *op cit*, p 54.
24. Howard Clinebell, *Growth Groups* (Abingdon: Nashville, TN, 1977), p 81.
25. Gordon MacDonald, *op cit*, p 73.
26. Anne Long, *Approaches to Spiritual Direction* (Grove: Bramcote, 1984), p 5.
27. Denis Duncan, article in *The Church of England Newspaper* (30th March 1984).
28. Charles Sibthorpe, *A Man under Authority* (Kingsway: Eastbourne, 1984), p 18.

Seconds Away!

by David Cormack

Are you winning or losing? If your life is too disorganised, or too demanding, or just not going anywhere—or even going so well that you want to keep it that way—then *Seconds Away!* can help.

'This text is more than just a book,' writes Dr David Cormack. 'I have designed it as an experience for you, an experience which will equip you to live your life in a manner which give more times of confidence, more times of satisfaction, more times of peace and rest.

Seconds Away! is a course in productive and effective living for leaders and readers of all ages and backgrounds. This could be one of the most important books you will ever buy—and one of the best investments.

'A book that can change your life—as it is changing mine.'
—Margaret Duggan, *Church Times*

David Cormack, formerly head of Training and Organisation Development at Shell International, draws upon his own extensive experience of management training and upon many other sources, particularly the Bible, for his cheerful and stimulating instruction in the art of leading a fuller, more satisfying life. He is now head of Cormack Consultancies, and a consultant in management training for MARC Europe. He is also author of *Team Spirit* and *Peacing Together*.

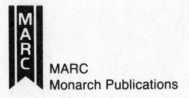

MARC
Monarch Publications

The Urban Christian

by Raymonde Bakke

Vast and terrible urban agglomerations house about half the population of the world.

'Modern urbanisation,' warns Ray Bakke, 'combines large-scale immigration from rural areas with exploding birth-rates. These cities have young populations with no history and without the constraints found in rural communities. *They are rootless, mobile, media-tuned, volatile. The peak of urban violence is yet to come in these flashpoint human aggregations.*'

This planet supports with difficulty, more than 290 cities with populations of over one million. Cities present particular challenges, and the churches are *not* ready to meet them, Ray Bakke insists. Churches need to recognise the huge potential of the cities, and to train people—urban missionaries—to live and minister and love the people there.

After an initial survey of world-class cities, Dr Bakke examines the fears of the churches; offers a biblical perspective on cities; details his own experience as a Baptist minister in downtown Chicago; and offers guidance for effective Christian witness in today's increasingly urban world. His impassioned presentation makes compulsive reading.

MARC
Monarch Publications